36^{58}

Happy Jack's Go Buggy
A Fighter Pilot's Story

Jack Ilfrey
with Mark S. Copeland

Happy Jack's Go Buggy

A Fighter Pilot's Story

Jack Ilfrey
with Mark S. Copeland

Schiffer Military/Aviation History
Atglen, PA

ACKNOWLEDGMENTS

Mark S. Copeland - Editor
Max Reynolds - Author and poet who helped write the original Happy Jack's Go Buggy in the summer of 1946
Eddie Rickenbacker
Royal Frey
John Stanaway
Winston Burdett, CBS correspondent
Ben Lyons, Combat Classroom of the Air

Stephen Grey - Owner of Classic Fighter Collection, Duxford, England
Roger Freeman
Len Deighton
John C. Valo
James H. Doolittle
Buddy Joffrion
Poet "The War Pony"

Book Design by Ian Robertson.

Copyright © 1998 by Jack Ilfrey.
Library of Congress Catalog Number: 98-85007

All rights reserved. No part of this work may be reproduced or used in any forms or by any means – graphic, electronic or mechanical, including photocopying or information storage and retrieval systems – without written permission from the copyright holder.
"Schiffer," "Schiffer Publishing Ltd. & Design," and "Design of pen and ink well" are registered trademarks of Schiffer Publishing, Ltd.

Printed in China
ISBN: 0-7643-0664-2

We are interested in hearing from authors with book ideas on related topics.

> Published by Schiffer Publishing Ltd.
> 4880 Lower Valley Road
> Atglen, PA 19310
> Phone: (610) 593-1777
> FAX: (610) 593-2002
> E-mail: schifferbk@aol.com
> Please write for a free catalog.
> This book may be purchased from the publisher.
> Please include $3.95 postage.
> Try your bookstore first.

CONTENTS

Foreword 6
Introduction 7

CHAPTER 1
The Early Years 8

CHAPTER 2
Bolero Mission: First mass flight of fighters across the North Atlantic to England- July 1942 17

CHAPTER 3
A New World and an Old World 25

CHAPTER 4
North Africa 40

CHAPTER 5
Stateside At Last 61

CHAPTER 6
Back to the Old Grind Again 64

CHAPTER 7
"It Finally Happened to Me, Too!" 73

CHAPTER 8
And Now The Buzz Bombs 86

CHAPTER 9
Back to Duty 88

CHAPTER 10
Two Ride A Mustang 95

CHAPTER 11
Russia 98

CHAPTER 12
Epilogue 102

Color Gallery 109
Appendix : Radio Interview with Winston Burdett to CBS, New York, March 21, 1943 123

Bibliography 124
Index 125

FOREWORD

Atom bomb and atom bomber, B-29 Super-Fortress and B-36 Super-Fortress—all will come and go, but in my opinion, the fighter pilot and the single-seat fighter plane will always have a prominent place in any war, be it in the air or on the ground.

Jack Ilfrey's description of his inner feelings, as well as facts, should be read by not only the youngsters of today and tomorrow, but by the soldiers, sailors, and aviators, as well as their relatives and friends, of World War II.

The speed, power, and armament of the fighter plane in World War II makes a World War I pilot, like myself, shudder and cringe, and, at the same time, be grateful for having been a fighter pilot of World War I. No doubt the boy fighter pilots of World War II shuddered and cringed at the thought of flying what they term "kites," which were the planes we used in World War I; but they must remember that while we had one-hundred-mile-per-hour planes, they had four-hundred-mile-an-hour planes; while we had two little pop-guns, they had six to eight, double the size and firing twice as rapidly, plus a cannon or two thrown in for good measure as offensive and defensive weapons.

There were literally thousands in the air—both enemy and friend—by comparison with the few in the air in World War I, multiplying, in my opinion, the hazards manifold.

What the fighter pilot will be, and what his type of plane will be in World War III—God forbid there be one—is difficult to foresee; but we can rest assured that the mixed feelings and admiration the pilots of World War II had for fighter pilots of World War I, because of the type of plane they were flying, will be just as great on the part of the fighter pilots of World War III for those of World War II.

Surely, then, no one dare miss reading Jack Ilfrey's book, because it is not only interesting reading matter, but enlightening as well.

Eddie Rickenbacker

Captain Eddie Rickenbacker—France 1918 (Credit - John M. Campbell Archives)

INTRODUCTION

The original 1946 manuscript was first published in 1978 in its entirety. Up until that time, over thirty years, I had been busy furthering my education and making a living and had become completely away from everything pertaining to W.W. II and almost every one I had known during those days.

Then after the book was out I started hearing from many friends and acquaintances, joined several organizations and started going to reunions.

I found it most rejuvenating talking over old times with many of my combat buddies and realized that friendships formed in combat are never forgotten.

I learned many things that I had forgotten and many other facts that I did not know when I wrote the first manuscript in 1946.

In 1982 I started editing the 20th Fighter Group Association's Newsletter "King's Cliffe Remembered" - (Our base in England). A great many first person stories and pictures have been sent to me for printing in the newsletter.

These stories are still coming direct from the horse's mouth, even though most all the horses are now out to pasture.

Therefore this printing will be revised and expanded and with many more pictures, and stories from the 1st and 20th Fighter Groups, 12th and 8th A.F..

We, now elderly, fighter Jocks believe our experiences should be written down for posterity in hopes that future generations will not have to go through what we did.

Getting the original manuscript off the closet shelf thirty-two years after it had been written.

1
THE EARLY YEARS

Houston, Texas, in 1920, was a pleasant place to be born and grow up. In that year it had a population of 106,667. Today, 1998, the population is 2,818,199.

My parents and I started out on the right track right away and remained that way until their deaths, father in 1960 and mother in 1987. We always had a good rapport, a good relationship, one of mutual trust. I never thought of or had to lie to them about anything. They understood and were very liberal with me.

One of my first recollections was of my mother's father, who came from England and spoke funny. He always had a parrot on his shoulder.

Another early recollection was my parents' 1918 Patterson Sports Roadster. Safety belts were unheard of so my mother used to tie me in with a rope.

Started school in the fall of 1926 - Woodrow Wilson Elementary. 1932 - Sydney Lanier Junior High School. 1935 - San Jacinto Senior High School. Along about this time I started working at *Henke and Pilott Grocery* Store at the corner of Travis and Tuam for 25 cents per hour. At the same time I had a Houston Post morning paper delivery route.

Graduated high school in the first class of the new high school, Mirabeau Lamar Senior High, in the spring of 1938.

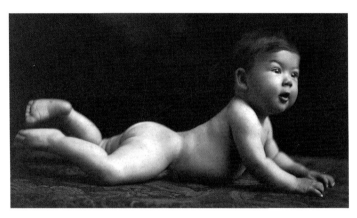

At seven months; picture was in the Rotogravure section of the *Houston Chronicle*.

At 16 months in the arms of my mother.

CHAPTER 1: The Early Years

My mother Grace in my parent's 1918 Patterson.

Enrolled in civilian training program at Texas A & M, 1940. Instructor Doug Beers (middle); I am at the left.

A. & M. Cooperates 100 Per Cent With CAA Training Plan

Winter - Spring 1940

Take First Flying Course

Since the Civil Aeronautics Authority launched its new program to train 20,000 men a year, many A. & M. students have accepted the chance to obtain first-hand instruction in handling a plane. Through the efforts of Dean of Engineering Gibb Gilchrist, A. & M. was selected as one of the schools where the new program would be carried out. A. & M. is now participating 100% in the program and is equipped with a flying field which promises to be one of the best in this section of the state.

To take part in the program it was necessary for the college to secure an airport that would meet the requirements of the C. A. A. Through cooperation with the city of Bryan a site was selected about two miles west of the college. The Cadette Aviation Company was awarded the contract to train students, and they have erected a large sheet-iron hangar at a cost of approximately $2,500. They have five planes used in student training. Three are Taylor-Craft and two Piper-Cubs. These planes develop fifty horsepower and have a cruising speed of 80 miles per hour.

Work is being done on the field by a non-student N. Y. A. group and the college has furnished some of its equipment to level the runways. The State Highway Department is planning to convert the county road, now passing near the airport, into a state highway connecting with the Caldwell road.

At present there are only two runways on the field but it is planned to develop three runways capable of landing any type of plane that might want to land here. A north-south runway is planned that will be 5,280 feet long and 500 feet wide. A group of civil engineers
(Continued on page 4)

In the plane above are seated two of the students taking the flight training program at A. & M. C. E. Tabor is in the rear cockpit, and J. M. Ilfrey at the controls. Both have soloed.

In the lower picture are standing left to right, Ilfrey, F. C. Thomas, J. M. Isbell; kneeling, left to right, Tabor, S. E. Brown and J. R. Propst. These are part of the forty students taking part in the flight training at A. & M.

Article from the Texas Aggie student newspaper.

Was an A and B student all through school. Was the first kid in the neighborhood allowed to drive the family car. This was before Texas had driver's licenses.

Worked all that summer and in the fall enrolled in *Texas A&M*. Asked for and was placed in A Troop Cavalry, Law Hall. They were still on horses. It cost $50.00 a semester to register, $30.00 a month room and board, all clothes were furnished.

The upperclassmen were mostly farmers and ranchers sons, small town country boys. They were delighted to see a few city boys in the Cavalry, thinking we would not know much about horses, and they could make fun of us. But they were wrong about me. The father of a good friend of mine in high school owned and operated a stable, and I learned a lot from them and became a fairly expert horseman.

The first test came soon enough, on our first maneuvers. A pre-W.W.I rifle was in a scabbard on our left side. A saber hung on the right side. Two bits were in the horse's mouth and four reins were held in the left hand. The right hand grasped a lance that was placed upright, mounted in a small leather cup by the right foot.

So off we go, column of twos, column of fours, etc. The horses seemed to know the orders better than we did. Then the fun comes when the leaders (seniors) start to march us through a heavily wooded area. You had to be quick to get the lance in a horizontal position. Then came the jumps. I seemed to be just as good as anyone else doing the jumps.

On other maneuvers, a squad of four, on horses, would lead a mule with a water cooled machine gun tied to its back. Then we would ford

Now an Army Flying Cadet.

In downtown Houston just before my leaving for cadet training.

the Brazos river and upon reaching the other side would dismount and set up the machine gun as quickly as possible.

The next year, as a sophomore, was a turning point in my life. In the fall of 1939 the Civilian Aviation Administration sponsored the first Civilian Pilot Training Program and selected over four hundred colleges as sites for the program in hopes of producing more than 10,000 new pilots. Texas A&M was one of the schools. More than 250 students applied for the 40 available slots in the first class. I was one of the lucky students chosen.

We started the class in January 1940 on a hastily prepared dirt strip with three Taylorcrafts and two Piper Cubs. I had a good instructor, Doug Beers, from Rochester, NY. He soloed me in 5 1/2 hours and I had no trouble finishing the required 35 hours to receive my private pilot license. My mother was my first passenger.

I had enjoyed my two years at A&M. No problems with grades, took easily the disciplines and regimentations of military training, even all the hazing during the first year. Made many friends. Was considered to be a Hail Fellow Well Met which continues to this day.

That summer of 1940 I had a job with Hughes Tool Company in Houston, at night, $65.00 per month. I relieved the two switchboard operators at 5pm and kept it open until midnight, taking orders from oil field operators.

Another thrill of a lifetime incident: Houston had always been proud of Howard Hughes. One late afternoon when I reported for work he put his head in the door and told one of the operators to stay on duty and told me to take his Auburn out and get it washed. Was I ever impressed. He was as swashbuckling as Errol Flynn.

In the fall I enrolled in the University of Houston. Applied and was accepted for the secondary Civilian Pilot Training Program. This time flying Fairchild PT-19s with Aviation Enterprises at Houston Municipal Airport, which still had shell runways. At the end of that semester, Feb. 1, 1941, I went over to Fort Sam Houston and Randolph Field, in San Antonio, passed all the examinations and was accepted in the US Army Air Corps Aviation Cadet Program. At that time, we needed two years of college credit to be accepted. Was told to go home and await further orders. They came around March 15th, telling me to report to Ryan Field Hemet, California, for primary cadet training. My folks and I were in mutual agreement that surely I had to be born at the right time.

However, 18 months later, while flying combat against the Germans, I was saying to myself, "what in the hell am I doing here?"

CHAPTER 1: The Early Years

Formal Cadet Photo taken at Hemet Field.

Hemet Field; Stearman PT-13 Primary Trainer.

Entrance gate to Moffett Field.

U.S. Army Air Corps Aviation Cadet Flight Training

My mother and one of her friends drove me out to Hemet, near March Field, California. Reported in, received uniforms, cadets wore blue gray, and room assignment. Four cadets in one half of a small cabin. We were now in the class of 41-I. The upperclassmen, 41-H, descended on us and started teaching correct military marching calisthenics and other disciplines. We marched everywhere, to the mess hall, ground school and back and forth to the flight lines. Shades of Texas A&M. Our instructors were civilians and again I had a good one, Jack Grady.

The Stearman PT13 was a fun plane to fly, a real seat of the pants aircraft. I already had around 200 hours of dual and solo flying time. All I had to learn here was to do it the army way. On my third flight with the instructor, Jack Grady, he told me, over the gosport, to do some slow rolls. I did a perfect 8 pointer. He told me to take it down and upon landing he got out and said, "It's all yours." Soloed the PT13 at 3:15 minutes.

For me, the training at this army primary school was just a repeat of my two civilian pilot training programs. However, approximately 50% of the class was washed out and most of them became bombardiers or navigators.

After 60 hours of flying time, we were transferred to Moffett Field at Sunnyvale, CA for basic training, flying the closed canopy Vultee BT13. We were now in a 100% military environment. Regimentation was stricter. We were housed in large bays in a permanent dormitory. Lt. Mode, my instructor, started teaching us formation flying. We were introduced to the Link Trainer to learn instrument flying. I for one did not like that little black box. Also did not like trying to learn Morse Code. But with patience and perseverance I was able to meet the requirements.

Jimmy Stewart, the actor, was stationed here at this time as a corporal. I can remember that one of our classmates was discovered to have epilepsy.

I was able to purchase a 1933 Ford convertible for $110.00. Now with a few friends we were able to see the sights of San Francisco and surrounding areas including the bar at the Spanish-style Hotel DeAnda in San Jose. Even in July, we found the rumble seat to be cold.

Treasure Island, San Francisco Bay; Boeing 314 *Pan American* Clipper "The China Clipper" in the background - August 1941.

With very few washouts, most of the class of 41-I completed our basic training at Moffett Field and were separated into two groups: multi-engine bomber pilot training, and single engine fighter pilot training. I was pleased to be selected for the latter. Cadet Tom Warrick and I took off in my old Ford in early October for Luke Field, near Phoenix, Arizona, for our advanced training in AT-6s. We made a mistake by going through Death Valley where the old Ford boiled over and cracked a head. We limped in to Luke just in time for the dedication ceremonies of the new field. Not a tree or a blade of grass was showing. Nothing but beautiful brown sand. Here we continued with close formation flying Link training and actual instrument flying in the AT-6. Some high altitude work using oxygen, and I believe some gunnery practice.

While in downtown Phoenix one weekend, I looked at a 1937 LaSalle that the car dealer was asking $375 for. I told him I had a '33 Ford to trade in and he said bring it in for him to look at. I forgot to tell him it wasn't running. The next weekend I had a friend push me all the way in to the car lot. About half a block before we got there, he gave me a real good shove and I coasted in to the parking lot and made motions of turning off the motor. The car did look good but when the dealer wanted to start the motor I told him the battery was dead. He didn't even look under the hood but told me to come on in and we'd make a deal.

Earlier I have said I was taught to be honest, but rationalized this by thinking I was no longer under my good parents thumb, and that I had heard that there was a little larceny in all car dealers and the fact that he was selling brand new Fords to the military for no down payment with an allotment. The LaSalle was a real good 100 mph car.

On Saturday night the 6th of December, several of us went to a dance and stayed over at the Westward Ho House hotel, which at that time was the largest building a few blocks out of downtown Phoenix on N. Central.

At mid-morning the next day, 7th December, 1941, we were awakened by loud voices and thumping in the halls with a loud

1933 Ford in front of Moffett Field Barracks - July 1941.

1937 LaSalle; Luke Field, Arizona - October 1941.

CHAPTER 1: The Early Years

Army Aviation Cadet Jack Ilfrey just before becoming a 2/Lt., Luke Field, Arizona - Early December 1941.

2/Lt. Jack M. Ilfrey - Luke Field - 12 December 1941.

In the cockpit of a North American P-64, Luke Field - December 1941.

My A-2 Leather Jacket shows the Indian Patch, 94th Pursuit Squadron; Long Beach - February 1942. Our squadron got the "Hat in the Ring" emblem back the following April.

"Captain Eddie" at Long Beach showing us pilots how to make deflection shots; I am on extreme left with my back to the camera.

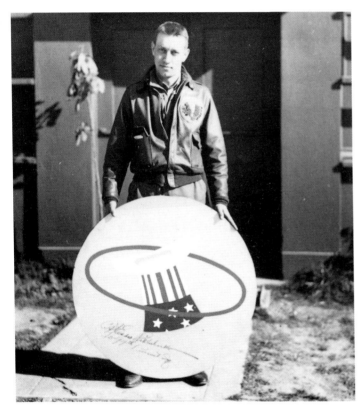

Captain Glenn Hubbard, Commanding Officer of the 94th "Hat in the Ring" Squadron, Long Beach California. The insignia was returned to the 94th Squadron, presented and signed by Eddie Rickenbacker.

Rickenbacker showing us how it's done. He was a great inspiration to us. Lt. Newell Roberts (left) and Lt. George Sutcliffe (right).

CHAPTER 1: The Early Years

With my 1940 Mercury Convertible; Long Beach, California - March 1942.

Long Beach, California - March 1942. On my left shoulder is the Croix De Guerre (Cross of Valor) awarded to the 94th Aero Squadron by the French Government in World War I.

knocking at our door and a loud voice saying, "Report to base immediately."

"What for?" No answer. So we turned over to go back to sleep - still hung over. In less than a minute the same loud knock, loud voice, adding, "Open it in 10 seconds, or we'll break it in."

"Wait until we get dressed."

"NOW!" the voice replied.

We complied and two M.P.s waited for us to get dressed, while they told us, "It's WAR!"

I believe most anyone alive on that day remembers where they were and what they were doing.

Five days later, 12 Dec. 1941, the class of 41-I graduated. Instead of elation, somberness prevailed. Hundreds of questions were going around. Nobody seemed to have any answers. We were restricted to base. To kill a little time, we flew a few P-43s and P-64s. The P-64 was a single seat souped up North American AT-6. The extra power made it a little tricky to fly.

Assigned to the 94th Pursuit Squadron 1st Pursuit Group

In 8 - 10 days orders started coming out and I was on a list to report to March Field and was assigned to the 1st Pursuit Group, flying P-38s, which had just recently flown out from Selfridge Field, Michigan. Six of us were assigned to the 94th Pursuit Squadron, now at N. Island Naval Airbase in San Diego flying defense patrols. The 71sts Squadron was based at Glendale - the 27th at Mines Field.

Utter confusion prevailed in southern California, the Japs were due any minute.

We were in awe of the P-38. It looked like a beautiful monster. We were also in awe of 1/LT Ralph Garman, commanding officer of the 94th Squadron, who later became C.O. of the 1st Fighter Group in N. Africa.

I was assigned to the flight of Lt. Newell Roberts, who had been in the 94th when they were the first outfit to be fully equipped with P-38s earlier that year - 1941. At first he seemed to be quite strict - all business - no foolishness. But later, after I had been flying his wing in combat, I developed respect and a great bond with him.

In those days we first read the flight manual over, several times. We walked around and around the P-38 with the flight leader. We were taught the proper procedures and fired up the engines. Practiced taxiing until we got the gallop out of it. Then we were ready for our first take off. No piggy backs in those days. It was the biggest thrill of my then young life. If you got it back on the ground, you were then a qualified P-38 pilot. Some didn't.

The N. Island Navy quarters and officers club were the best we had seen at that time. The Navy officers thought we were a rag-tag bunch due to the many combinations of uniforms we could wear.

The Navy had a strange (to us) procedure for take offs and landings. On top of the control tower was a tall pole with four large different color balls mounted on the pole. The arrangement of the

Left to right: Lt. Charles Shelton, 94th Squadron Engineer Officer, movie starlet Lorraine Ilfrey (my cousin), and me.

colors told you what direction to use for take offs and landings. Along comes one of our pilots, Everett Umphries, on take off and knocked the balls off the tower. We heard that an admiral hurt himself when he jumped from the tower. We didn't know if this was why we were moved to Long Beach or not, but thought that it was probably because N. Island was becoming very crowded. In any event, 1/LT Glenn Hubbard had just taken over the 94th and we moved to Long Beach Municipal Airport on 9 Feb. 1942. We pilots established our quarters in a hangar on cots.

We continued our submarine patrols but the only thing I ever saw was a couple of whales. We did tow target practice over the ocean. Dive bombing practice up at dry Lake Muroc, before it became Edwards Air Force Base.

GETTING CLOSER TO COMBAT
In late April 1942, we picked up from the Lockheed factory in Burbank our new P-38-F1s which were fully combat operational. We continued our patrols and training. Even though it was forbidden, we took delight in buzzing the swimmers all along the southern California coast. Nothing was ever done about it, because the ones in charge thought it was good for the morale of the public.

On May 18th, we knew something was up because we were ordered to fly to Dow Field, Bangor, Maine, to stage with the 97th Bomb Group - B-17-Es. But for what?

We started practicing formation flying with the B-17s. A flight of four P-38s tucked in close on the wings of the B-17. This reduced our speed, making it harder to fly the P-38.

On June 7th we were recalled to the West Coast because of the Battle of Midway in the Pacific. However, the 94th SQ only got as far as Charlotte, NC, before being sent back to Dow Field. War jitters were becoming very prevalent. Finally, we received orders from Headquarters Eighth AF Fighter Command at Grenier Field, Manchester, NH., dated June 25, 1942, sending us on the Bolero Mission. The what mission?

2

THE BEGINNING OF A LONG JOURNEY
THE BOLERO MISSION

For extraordinary achievement while participating in a mass movement of Single-Seater Fighter airplanes from July 4, 1942 to July 25, 1942, over an extremely hazardous, newly established air route involving long over water flights under very uncertain weather conditions...flight was of great military importance...successful performance reflects highest credit on the military forces of the United States...

Citation for the awards of the first Air Medal in the 8th AF World War II given to the three squadrons of the First Fighter Group—from General Orders Number 46, by command of Major General Spaatz.

Leaving the States
July 4, 1942

It gave you a funny feeling to be leaving the United States on the Fourth of July. Funny...well, because this was Independence Day and here we were on our way to Labrador, the first stop on a long journey, to keep our independence.

As our P-38's climbed higher into the Maine sky that day at noon, I remembered an old, beat-up car I used to drive to high school, and I thought of my initiation at Texas A. & M. College...and how scared I was—and the panic inside me now was something like the feeling I had experienced as a freshman. Suddenly, I wanted a chocolate soda.

At Goose Bay, Labrador - July 6, 1942; the mosquitoes were as big as Stukas!!!

Everett Humphries - Goose Bay, Labrador

Iceberg In fjord.

We were flying along in groups of four and it was a beautiful sight to see four P-38s being led by their mother-ship, a B-17. Dick McWherter was not too far behind me and there was "Bugs" Lentz. I don't know what they were thinking about, but it wouldn't be far wrong if I said Paris, Texas.

Dick and "Bugs" talked about Paris a lot. Dick was full of life. He liked everybody and everybody liked him. He loved dancing and food and girls. I like to remember Dick dancing away on one of our last nights in Bangor before shoving off.

We didn't know much then but we learned fast.

I thought of my home town down on the Texas Gulf Coast. Houston was a nice town. There was plenty of rain and plenty of sunshine, too. There were things to do. There was a bay where you could go swimming and have fun with a boat. We owned a shack on the bay shore and my father was probably there, free of his duties at the bank. My mother would be taking it easy on the front porch, as she usually did on holidays. Houston seemed far, far away.

Colonel Ben Kelsey was making the trip with us. Kelsey had been Chief Test Pilot at Lockheed's in California, and he had believed in the P-38. He had fought for it and finally perfected it. The P-38 was a wonderful ship. It went a long, rugged way toward winning the war.

And Ben was a swell guy. We all liked him and were glad he made the trip with us—the trip that Washington had started planning back in March, 1942, when we were losing men and ships in the Atlantic.

Airplanes were needed quickly and in large numbers overseas. Some higher-up in Washington wanted to know how fighter planes and more bombers could be delivered to the places where they were so urgently needed. Bombers had been flown overseas, a few at a time, but never fighter planes, and I think it was Gen. H. H. ("Hap") Arnold who told the higher-up that the airplanes would have to be flown over. General Arnold had no more than made this remark when President Roosevelt telephoned and asked the same question. This, only 15 years after Charles Lindbergh's first solo flight across the North Atlantic (May 1927).

The almost impossible idea caught on. Flying fighter planes over the Atlantic had never been done before. There were great difficulties to be overcome and one difficulty presented more problems than all the rest. It was something you couldn't do anything about: the weather.

The route was dangerous all the way. There were winds to be bucked at 150 miles per hour. There were no procedures for obtaining data on the weather. One country we were to touch had no radios. Airdromes were in the process of being constructed and sketchy at best. And there were enemy planes over some of the territory we were to pass. It was said that the closeness to the North Pole at one place on our way would make a fighter's compass collapse. The P-

94th pilots on an iceberg in the fjord at Bluie, Greenland, July 1942.

Ilfrey, Widen, Humphrey on an ice cap above Bliue West 1, Greenland, with head protection from mosquitos, or what we termed as "Stukas!"

CHAPTER 2: The Beginning of a Long Journey - The Bolero Mission

94th Squadron P-38s parked at Reykjavik, Iceland.

38 did not have all of the complicated equipment needed for navigating; however, belly tanks for extra gasoline had just been perfected, each tank holding 150 gallons.

There was no doubt. We were the experiment, the guinea pigs, the real beginning of the Eighth Fighter Command. But we knew nothing. We had never heard of these plans. We did not know where we would eventually land, and we had no idea what our job would be.

There was one thing we were glad later we didn't know. A national magazine had shrewdly guessed and published the details of our epic flight. Our enemies all over the world knew our route. It was good we didn't know. The less you know when you are going off to war, the better off you are. It is not well to anticipate too much.

Nearly all the problems of our flight were solved by Brig. Gen. Frank ("Monk") Hunter. He had not been an ace in World War I for nothing, and his was the genius behind the Eighth Air Force. "Monk" had briefed us for the trip in Maine and had gone ahead to meet us. He had real knowledge and he inspired confidence.

The weather was fine. The Saint Lawrence looked peaceful and the Canadian woods gave you a tranquil feeling. It was hard to remember that you might not come back. And most of us didn't come back.

There was no wind at all as we turned into Goose Bay, Labrador. The sky was a hazy blue, and lying right off the coast were the first icebergs we had ever seen. We were getting closer...

It was exactly 4:30 in the afternoon when we landed at the airport in Goose Bay, which was just a clearing near the edge of the bay. Off in the distance was a pine forest. The atmosphere was "North Woodsey." Almost any moment I expected to see a "mountie" on his horse—maybe I'd been seeing too many movies back in Texas.

From the time we got out of our airplanes we were attacked by hundreds of insects, gnats, mosquitoes, and many other little animals with whom I was not acquainted. I noticed later that the natives, who were dreary looking and ragged, did not seem to be bothered by the bites of the insects. It might have been that the smell of the inhabitants discouraged the insects from biting too deep or too long.

Of course, we expected to see Eskimos all over the place and we saw none. Life seemed pretty dull and rugged for the few Indians and white people we saw. There was nothing but icy water, insects, and sand. The natives fished and trapped for a living. Their homes were bleak-looking wooden huts, and there was no sign of cheerfulness anywhere.

After we had put our airplanes to bed, we had something to eat. And not too much either, remembering this was back in 1942 when supplies were coming through slowly, if at all. We quartered down for the night in a crude building that was just one big room.

We were too restless to sleep much that night. Some of us sat on the double-deck bunks and wrote letters home. Bull sessions were going on in every corner of the room, with a big dice game in the middle of it.

On Our Way to Greenland
July 6, 1942

We stayed in Goose Bay for a day and a half. By ten o'clock of the second morning we had eaten breakfast, received our briefing for the next lap of the journey, and were in the air again. The weather was favorable when we started out. There was a high overcast and everything went well for the first hour.

We were all a little sleepy, a little excited, and a shade scared. Here we were, the fighter pilots and the bomber pilots, blazing the trail for other flights to come. It sort of awed you and at the same time frightened you. You didn't seem quite real. You lost your identity. Every now and then I had to remind myself that my name was Jack Ilfrey, that I was not yet twenty-two years old. I was on my way to fight a war. War. It was hard to think about that.

The Icebergs were pretty in the sunlight and gave you the impression that they were floating along the Labrador coast. We were flying low and could see the coast well. It was specked with deep bays, excellent harbors, and many outlying islands. The scene below was peaceful, but it was peace with a desolation that was not quieting.

Our group had left Labrador on the strength of a broadcasted weather report, and we had not waited for the return of the weather ship from its inspection trip. It began to get murky, and we could not see the other flights. (In the meantime, the weather ship had returned to Labrador and radioed the B-17s to turn back, with the fighter pilots. The B-17 we were flying with did not receive this report because of faulty radio reception and the static conditions peculiar to that part of the world.) Our flight was "Tom Cat Black."

The weather got worse and worse as we flew on. Finally, the pilot of the B-17 radioed to us that we had better close in tight on him, as it appeared to be getting thick up ahead. Jim Harmon, who was our flight leader, did not close up in time and we lost him. But the other three of us closed in tight on the B-17 and flew on into the thick overcast. We tried to fly over the cloud bank and clipped it up to 25,000 feet, but we still couldn't break out.

Then we started picking up ice. The B-17 had de-icers on its wings, but there was nothing on our fighter planes with which to fight ice. When the fighter plane was in a warmer region of air, the ice did not form enough to cause trouble. All this time we were flying on instruments, in the constantly deepening fog.

Bennett, the B-17 pilot, decided to fly on farther. His navigator said he knew where we were, that we were not far from Greenland. This was a relief to our chilled bodies and minds. In about thirty minutes—it seemed like hours—the B-17 radio operator made contact with the base in Greenland, and we were told by Greenland the weather was clear at the base there. We all breathed more easily. It was a wonderful feeling to know where we were and that clear weather was ahead. We flew for another hour on instruments and broke out of the overcast at last.

And then we saw a most beautiful spectacle. Greenland, an unbroken ice cap, was still some 100 miles away, but we were able to make out the icebergs sparkling in the blue greenish water. It really looked like Greenland was only about 15 miles away, from our height of 25,000 feet, when it was actually about 100 miles. Distances are deceiving when the weather is clear at a great height, and you see things from 25,000 feet high, it is as though you are looking at a map.

Our tenseness went away. We shouted out, giving great whoops of joy. I pulled over to the side and did a loop. One of the other fighters slid into a slow roll. You don't know what happiness is until you've been in an airplane, thousands of feet up in the air, with the wind buffeting you around at 150 miles an hour. You don't think about dying. You think about living. And getting the hell out of the storm.

Coming down lower, we saw that the shoreline was not covered by the ice cap, and we could see quite a distance inland and the beginning of the ice cap.

We had been thoroughly briefed about landing at the airdrome in Greenland. Now I saw the reasons for such complete coaching. The airfield consisted of just one steel strip, which was located some forty miles inland, near the ice cap. There was only one way you could get to the landing strip; fly up a large fjord to a point where the fjord spread out several miles wide.

We had to circle low, let our wheels down, and approach the end of the strip that was nearest the water. There was no other way to land. You had to come in over the water and land on the bottom of the strip, run up hill several thousand yards to the end of the runway, which was 100 feet up from the bottom. When you took off you merely turned around and ran down the strip, out over the fjord, and followed it down to the open ocean. The glacier began at the back of the airfield and stretched toward the middle of the ice cap, rising to a height of over 9,000 feet.

When we put our feet on firm ground, it was 3:30 in the afternoon. It was hard to realize we had been flying for only five and one-half hours. It seemed like an eternity since we had left Labrador at ten o'clock in the morning. We felt more mature. An airplane, darkness, a storm, and uncertainty can help you to grow up in a hurry. You did not think about these things consciously, but the subconscious helped a lot.

I was suddenly exhausted. I wanted food. I wanted a bed. I wanted sleep. And I didn't want to think. That was something I could not escape, however. I had to think about Harmon who did not close in with us. I had to think about the rest of the bunch.

We tried to get Labrador by radio and failed. There was to be no calming down yet, no settling down.

The beans and the coffee and toasted bread tasted good. We were in the middle of eating when Harmon came flying in and we all rushed out to the strip to meet him. He was all right. With no B-17 to guide him, he had done an amazing job of flying through the overcast and the storm and coming into Greenland and finding the airdrome.

Ten minutes after Harmon arrived, two more P-38s flew in—Dick McWherter and Williams— and they reported a duplicate of Harmon's experience, except they had heard the radio report from the base in Greenland to our B-17, saying the weather was clear.

Out of the whole squadron of twenty-four airplanes and accompanying B-17s, only six P-38s and one B-17 had landed in Greenland that day.

The arrival of Harmon, McWherter, and Williams changed our mood entirely—at least for a while. All three men were swamped with compliments on their skillful flying. Until you've heard high praise in the air force, you've heard nothing. Everybody was excited and everybody talked at once. Good friendship flowed like warm sunshine after a rain. There were the moments you remembered, but there were other moments you didn't want to remember. Sometimes you couldn't remember at all. It was just space in your mind.

We calmed down long enough to eat again and get in our bunks. But we had a hard time going to sleep. We were thinking of our comrades-in-arms who were still missing. As it turned out, all the rest had heard the weather ship's report and turned back to Labrador. We knew nothing that night, and eventually came the release into a dreamless, exhausted sleep.

Night Becomes Day
At first I thought it was morning when I woke up. Bright sunlight was everywhere. A glance at my watch, however, told me it was only 11:00 p.m. I had an odd feeling. Here it was eleven o'clock at night, the sun was shining brightly, and here I was, in a completely strange world.

What was I doing here? The fog in my brain disappeared and I remembered there was a war. I was on my way to war. And again that funny feeling—a feeling that was to follow me over a large part of the earth's area. You can't describe the feeling. You can't talk about it. You just feel it.

And my next thought, ironically, was pure, first edition American: Let's go sight-seeing. If we Americans are born with a national characteristic, it's the idea that we must see all new things as quickly as possible and in the most expensive manner possible. It would never occur to us to take things slowly, absorb the atmosphere a little more, and come back, not just typical (and offensive) tourists, but people with more understanding of what they have heard and seen.

In no less typical American fashion, I noisily roused a few of my grumbling and sleepy buddies. The tourist feeling caught on like a prairie wildfire, and we dressed in no time flat and stepped out into this new world.

A new world indeed, a bleak world, a world that was a million miles from nowhere. The contrast struck us hard. We didn't say much. We were pretty dumb. This moment passed as quickly as it

CHAPTER 2: The Beginning of a Long Journey - The Bolero Mission

had come and the desire to explore, see things, and comment on them was as strong as ever.

We walked down to the end of the runway, on the edge of the fjord, and found a Coast Guard cutter tied up there. I don't need to say that we "commandeered" a lifeboat off the cutter. We were going fishing, fishing in the Arctic. That was something to write home about.

The men who were stationed at the base were still milling around and helped us to find our bait—little pieces of tin that would shine and attract the fish. We never thought we would be using our jungle kits for fishing in the Arctic when we dug out the hooks and lines. The jungle kit was man's best friend on occasion, and it was made right into the parachute, which contained our small rubber boat, the dinghy, all tightly folded into a square package. The packing was a masterpiece.

The jungle kit was a small variety store and, among other things, included:
A large machete (knife)
Small watertight cylinders that contained matches, purifying water tablets, and halozone tablets
Concentrated malt tablets
Concentrated chocolate bars
A small rubber water bottle
Morphine syrettes
Benzedrine tablets

When we got all set, we rowed out to the icebergs. It was hard to fight down the feeling that this was fishing clear out of this world...fishing among icebergs.

The icebergs were something special. One was about the size of the Houston Art Museum, if you can picture that, and it was a glistening white. You could see far down into the green water, and on looking closer you found that the base of the iceberg was about twice the size of the top of the berg. There was a certain kind of classic beauty about the icebergs, a certain kind of fascination. You thought of the Titanic, treachery, and a lot of other things. When you looked at one, you felt insignificant, that you did not matter.

We must have fished for an hour or more and finally fishing became routine. We caught small dogfish—something like mackerel—as fast as we could pull them in. It was past midnight, and catching so many fish was no longer sport. It was a bore but it was an experience to remember—sitting in a lifeboat in the middle of the night, in the Arctic, with sunlight playing all around, fishing.

That night, or should I say morning, as we walked back to the barracks, I realized perhaps for the first time, just how small the world had been in which I had lived. This might have been the beginning of my international thinking. It dawned on me that no man, no nation, can be complete by himself or itself.

The Second Day in Greenland
This time it was really morning by the clock when we crawled out of our bunks, and there was nothing to do except wait for the weather to clear and to wait for the pilots who were still in Labrador to join us. So we decided to go on another sight-seeing tour. We had heard there was a little Eskimo village on the other side of the fjord, and again we "borrowed" the Coast Guard lifeboat.

As we walked up the trail to the village, my first impression was smell, more smell, and then one big smell that knocked out all the other smells. Sid Pennington said the natives had an odor like a paper mill. I think he was right—maybe two paper mills and one or two sewage disposal plants thrown in.

Of course, we looked for igloos right away, and still we saw no igloos. I felt a little resentful toward writers I had read, and wished they had been more realistic in describing the Eskimo. All we saw were shacks in the process of decaying or falling down. There was desolation here, hopelessness, and, it seemed to me, eternal poverty.

Besides the Eskimo, we saw a few Danes, and for all practical purposes, the Danes had become Eskimo. The whole lot of them were dirty and ragged, and when you came up close to them, you had to turn your head quickly and think of something to keep from vomiting. It's odd how powerfully smell can affect the stomach.

The adult natives had no curiosity and did not bother to look at us as we passed. They had lived too long in this godforsaken place and their perceptions had been dulled beyond redemption. They were human robots. They did not feel and they did not think. For all I know, they could not hear or see, and, most certainly, they could not smell.

One look (and smell) at their clothes told you the reindeer skins and the sealskins had been worn for years, without once having them off. From the outline, I would say the clothes were put on the Eskimos when they were half grown, and the same clothes went to the grave with them.

The women were lifeless. They moved slowly, without seeming intent, interest, or purpose. It was difficult to imagine the sex life of the Eskimos, and the full significance came to me again, when I saw the children, that Nature takes care of everything, even in Greenland.

The Eskimo, in general, is dark and his skin oozes with oil. It may be whale oil or cod liver oil—I don't know—but most likely it is cod liver oil, his only fortification against the cold and the other more personal elements. Here our education began with the "handout," which was to pursue us wherever we went. The Eskimo children were not so sluggish as their parents and succeeded by the sign language and quaint gestures in begging candy from us. Maybe candy should be a universal language, and perhaps we should capitalize more on its distribution around the world. It sells good will.

We wouldn't have been good Americans if we had not looked for something to buy or trade, and we did look, carefully and long, but there was nothing to buy, nothing to barter for, and nothing to carry away as a souvenir. We left the Eskimo village disgusted. We had been gypped, no souvenirs, but we had a memory of wretchedness that we would never be able to consign to forgetfulness. The remembrance made you grateful for Crane plumbing, Hollywood, and nickel-and-dime stores.

Departure for Indigo
We took off at 3:30 the next morning from Bluie West One for Indigo, the code name for Iceland. Before the takeoff, however, we received a report that a German plane had been seen. After the alert,

we flew on several short patrols, but not a German plane was to be seen anywhere. We breathed more easily.

The six hours from Greenland to Iceland passed quickly and uneventfully. Good weather favored us all the way. I felt relaxed. The hike to the ice cap had had something to do with that. The relaxation that follows the tiring-out of the body and sore muscles is good.

When we landed at the airdrome near Reykjavik, we found General "Monk" waiting to greet us. It was good to see him and his imposing mustache. No time was lost in briefing us and giving us breakfast. The food was better than in Greenland and our quarters were Nissen huts, which were far more comfortable than the shack in Greenland. Here was a touch of civilization and one was learning to be grateful for things like that.

In record time, we were in our bunks and went sound asleep. We slept until seven o'clock that night. We got up refreshed, determined to see Reykjavik, and to find adventure.

At briefing that morning we had been told not to eat Icelandic foods and more especially the milk, which was supposed to be full of tubercular germs. We had also received the usual warnings about women, how to conduct ourselves as officers, and so on. It might be in order to say right here that our experiences in Reykjavik would have pleased even the intellectual Plato...

However we had pictured Iceland, it was not like that, and Reykjavik was unlike any of our conceptions. The name "Iceland" had placed a picture in our minds and whether we expected to see ice dripping from the housetops, I don't know. We saw no ice but we did see modern paved streets, automobiles running around, drug stores, beer parlors, pretty (and well-formed) girls, and, most surprising of all, taxicabs. Somehow you just didn't think of taxicabs careening around in Iceland—or at least I didn't. We hailed the first cab we saw and drove through some fine parks, looked at Reykjavik's good harbor, and saw the university. I observed that while the architecture of the homes was modern, nearly all of the houses had a squareness about them, which was not typical of houses back home, and this gave the town an atmosphere that recalled the medieval history you once studied.

The G.I. has a specially patented instinct for finding the right place, and it wasn't long before we discovered the Hotel Borg, which was a small place with a nice cocktail bar, and, again, to our amazement, an orchestra. The cocktail bar was dark and subdued and the Icelanders sat around drinking quietly—somewhat different from the American way of imbibing. The one percent tasteless beer we drank did not help to improve our spirits, so we smiled at the girls who were seated at the next table, and they looked at us. No smiles—nothing happened. Another clear and plain contrast to another American way of life. We felt pretty low and when the orchestra played good old U.S.A. tunes, our minds wandered. It's curious how familiar music affects you in a foreign country. Curious, too, how you can feel sad and happy practically at the same time.

Our waiter spoke excellent English, and he must have taken pity on our solitary state because he told us that if we wished to dance with the girls we had smiled at we must ask them three times, and then all would be well. I wondered aloud then if this three-times custom applied to everything else. One by one we went over and asked the girls three times if they cared to dance with us. The repetition made us feel pretty silly, but the system worked. Soon the girls were smiling and we were using the sign language hell-bent-for breakfast, and I broke out one of my carefully hoarded fifths of Four Roses I had brought from the States and concealed in my P-38. The Four Roses worked wonders.

The Icelandic girls were good dancers and good-looking blondes, with fresh complexions, and an animation that built morale.

When the orchestra played "Deep in the Heart of Texas," we let everybody know we were from Texas. It was hard to convince the Icelanders, however, that we were from the Lone Star State, as they thought of Texans as being bow-legged, wearing cowboy boots, and carrying guns on their hip. This, of course, brought on a big discussion, with all kinds of English being flung around, and the natives' accent made the English language interesting and quaint. While the girls in our party could not speak English, they helped us in trying to convince the Icelanders that we were just as surprised at them as they were at us, and after this, it wasn't long before the atmosphere in the cocktail bar was more Texan than Icelandic.

The bar closed at midnight, and when we walked outside into the bright, blazing sunlight, it was too much. Here we were, tight, in a lively mood, mellowed by the soft lights in the bar and the Icelandic blond beauties, suddenly slapped in the face by broad daylight. Everything was spoiled. You could feel the petals from the Four Roses withering fast. The girls left us and our low spirits increased.

Two big Danish policemen came forward and helped us find a taxicab. They must have seen the reaction on our faces and felt sorry for us.

We are Introduced to "Honey Buckets"

Our education was to include many things as time went along, one being an exposure to all sizes and all types of outhouses. When you have had such a wide sitting acquaintance with outhouses as I have, you achieve a profound respect for the American bathroom and its luxurious privacy.

These places became known to us under the general term of "honey buckets," and in Iceland we saw our first "honey bucket." Comfort and efficiency never occurred to the builders of these outhouses. The Icelandic carpenters simply took a small space, laid a board, and placed a five-gallon can beneath the board, and once a day a civilian would arrive in a little donkey cart and make the collections. Often you would be sitting on the "honey bucket," thinking about nothing in particular, when he would jerk the can from under you through an opening in the rear. No enemy ever made you jump faster. Sometimes you would knock the can over accidentally. If you had sensibilities, you had to get rid of them.

At this time a squadron of P-39s were stationed in Iceland for defense, and the boys told us that a great many Icelanders were still pro-Nazi, and I had observed this attitude to some degree that evening in the Hotel Borg. One of the men told us when the first American troops arrived in Iceland, the natives had rushed down to the docks, crying "Heil Hitler!" They had mistaken our new helmet, which had just come out, for the Nazi headpiece.

CHAPTER 2: The Beginning of a Long Journey - The Bolero Mission

The Germans had established themselves well in Iceland before we came. They had built the University in Reykjavik and had started constructing the airdrome, which we finished. More important than everything else, the Germans had succeeded in making the natives Nazi-minded. I believe the Germans succeeded because they left nothing to chance. Their propaganda proved that.

The First Kill
August 14, 1942
Our 27th Squadron was left in Iceland for defense protection. We heard of this later and were very proud that the 1st Fighter Group scored first.

A report went out that a German Focke-Wulf—"Kurier" (Focke Wulf FW-200)—was over Iceland. Lightning struck the airdrome and before anybody could think twice, Major Weltman was in his P-38, tearing over the airdrome and charging the German's four-motored long-range bomber with his guns. And the Germans matched Weltman for quickness. When Weltman closed in, the Nazi gunners made direct hits on the Lightning's armament assembly, making the four guns on the P-38 useless. Then one of the plane's engines stopped, and Weltman made for the airdrome, knowing he was fighting a hopeless battle. By now another P-38, which was piloted by Elza Shahan, and a P-40 were in the air and getting in position to attack the German plane. Shahan made a pass at the enemy bomber, and with the P-40 closing in, they knocked out the Focke-Wulf's left inboard engine.

Action came fast. Shahan went into a chandelle, returned to position, and came in close for a side shot instead of a direct shot. He was within less than 100 yards of the German bomber when he pressed his button and let go. There was no gunner on the side of the bomber that was hit, and the four streams of .50-caliber tracer, incendiary, and armor-piercing bullets spelled the end of the German Focke-Wulf. After firing, Shahan planned to dive below the bomber, but the German plane blew up so quickly that all he could do was to go through the thick debris that was flying in the air. This was pretty dangerous, but he came through all right, even though his P-38 was scarred plenty. Shahan was the first American Air Force pilot in the European Theatre of Operation to knock out a German plane in World War II, and for that he got the Silver Star.

The Last Lap
July 25, 1942
The weather was nice and cool when we left Iceland on the last lap of the flight, and we were glad it was summertime and not winter, with wind whirling around you at the rate of 150 miles per hour.

Flying over the North Atlantic is never too much fun, even in the best weather. It's easy to get lost in that immense stretch of fog and water, and there is a bigness about the Atlantic Ocean that awes and scares you when one of those heavy overcasts wraps itself around you. It's then when your best friend is the B-17 that leads your plane, sets you on the course again, and takes care of you as long as the engines hold out.

Our route was to take us from Iceland to Stornaway, on the Isle of Lewis, in the Hebrides, and it seemed to me that we flew for hours without getting anywhere. I was numb from looking at dense fog, fighting squalls and storms. Lieutenant Rimke, the leader of our flight, finally asked Cronkhite, the B-17 pilot, where we were, and Cronkhite said he didn't know!

At least two more hours went by. We could not see the sun and our course was changed constantly in order to miss the rain squalls and the thunderheads that were still pursuing us. Cronkhite radioed that he didn't know the way back to Iceland, and Rimke said we might as well continue on the same course.

What did I think about all this time? Just one thing: Where in the hell was I? That's all. Don't believe the stuff you've read about what men think when they're lost. I've talked with too many pilots, and the only thought they have is to get out of the storm and find some place, any place, to land. You just want to know where you are. If there's a feeling about being lost, it's like you are suspended in space. Not nice and entirely too celestial.

We spotted a hole in the clouds and going down a little lower, we saw land below, and all you could say to yourself was: My God! Land! Was it England, Iceland, Germany, France, or Norway?

Clarence Rimke went down to investigate and when he came back up he said we were over the northern Irish coast, according to his charts. Just about that time we saw two fighters, which turned out to be British Spitfires, and we made radio contact with them at once. They told us they were running low on gas but would return to the base and send us help.

While we were waiting for help to arrive, we contacted several radio stations in Scotland. We felt better. There is nothing like human contact. Take it from whatever point of view you like, there's still nothing like it.

We were flying quite low over the Irish Sea and knowing we had little gasoline left, the waiting became agonizing. When the twin-engine Beaufighters came to lead us in at last, we learned that we would fly into Ayr, Scotland, on the Firth of Clyde.

Our P-38s had barely landed on the RAF airfield when the heavy fogs started rolling in. Our gasoline tanks were drained to the last drop. We had been in the air eight hours that day. Our hands trembled and we were soaking wet from the water that had accumulated in the cockpits; our eyes were bloodshot and our legs literally wobbled as we walked. Dead men on feet that still somehow propelled—that was us. This was the kind of glamour you don't see on the silver screen.

Scotch and Scottish Girls
We were late for dinner, of course, and the RAF mess hall was almost deserted when we walked in. There were a few British officers lingering over their tea and they came across the room and greeted us in a reserved though friendly way. Then my eye caught the trim Scottish waitress coming toward us. Her smile did things for you. You felt like celebrating. And we did. Somebody produced a bottle of Scotch, and we drank a toast to the waitress. The British officers were amazed at this but said nothing and I noticed later that the Britishers seemed to ignore the waitresses completely. The poor gals didn't exist as far as the British officer was concerned.

The food was good, the Scotch was better, and the waitress's Scottish burr entranced us. She was certainly a queen for that evening, and she had probably never been talked to so much before. I wouldn't be an American if I didn't add she liked the attention, too.

Although we had not really seen anything of Ayr, we started comparing Scotland with the U.S. We judged nearly everything at that time by food and women, and I still think these are pretty good points of comparison. If both food and women are in the highest degree, the country is bound to be all right.

We had a little trouble getting used to the waitress's Scottish burr, and while her voice was crisp, it was a soft crispness and clear. When she asked Everett Umphrey if he cared for "sweets," he misunderstood, not realizing she meant dessert, and told her (looking silly) that she was certainly sweet herself. We roared because Everett was deadly serious.

After dinner we walked around a bit. The Scotch whiskey had done wonders for us. It was still daylight, as darkness does not come until about 11:30 P.M. during the summer in Scotland. There were quaint little bridges across the canal from the airdrome, and, for no good reason, I thought of a movie I had seen—*The Tale of Two Cities*. Scotland had an old world atmosphere, and I suddenly wished I could remember more history. The woman who used to teach me history back in Houston marveled at my ability to pass examinations. I had a system then but it was a system that left no remembrance later. I did not know it but my capacity for being a student was going to deepen and my horizons were going to widen. And it wasn't going to be long, either. I had no foreknowledge that my curriculum was to contain courses that no college could offer.

We were still in our old flying clothes and boots and we were still a little wet. Around midnight we turned in, and by that time the blackout was complete. It was our first initiation—our first real initiation. The blackout made you feel grim—and aware.

I didn't sleep that night, and I don't think anyone else did. The stimulation of the whiskey had worn off and we were too tired to relax. Somehow the blackout worried me. It stirred up a lot of thinking. I was near the end of a long journey. There was the future ahead of me, a future that I knew nothing about. I had been on an epic trip across two oceans, four countries. I had grown up a little, matured a little. I had learned what it means to be afraid.

It's funny when you spend a whole night analyzing yourself. It's funny the thoughts you have. One thing I thought about was a girl in Houston I'd like to marry when the war was over. I knew the chances were against a successful marriage in wartime. You should be fully grown up when you get married. Your mentalities have got to match, and when a man goes to war, his mentality changes sometimes. Because of war, his thinking may become all the deeper and all the richer, or it may not. It depends on factors you cannot control.

Lying in my bunk, I recalled the time when I worked for Aviation Enterprises in Houston, absolutely carefree. Commercial flying was a far cry from war then. I was taking the college Civilian Pilot Training Program course at the University of Houston. We had already completed over 200 hours of flying time and had more than the necessary two years of college work to enter the air force.

Events that came to pass reminded me, in a personal way, of Luke, and our own "Hat-in-the-Ring" Squadron in World War II proved itself to be as much of a pioneer as it was in the First World War. We had a good many firsts in England and other places, but Rickenbacker's 94th Squadron was the first American squadron to go over the enemy's lines. His squadron was the first to bring down and destroy an enemy airplane, and his men brought down the last German airplane that fell in World War I.

So many things stood out that morning in Scotland and popped into my mind for no good reason: I recalled how the enlisted men had told the girls in Phoenix that we cadets had been quarantined because of venereal disease, and that we could be singled out and easily recognized by the blue uniforms we wore. Shortly afterwards the blue uniform was discarded but the shame remained. When I received my wings five days after Pearl Harbor, I was a member of the first graduating class in wartime.

December 12, 1941. I will never forget that day. I was a second lieutenant. I was something special.

Something special...it's good I fell asleep at that moment. England awaited me, as did many other things that were not very special, in any man's language.

3

A NEW WORLD AND AN OLD WORLD

When we landed at the RAF Airdrome in Kirton-in-Lindsey in Lincolnshire, the welcome that greeted us was something that cannot be described, at least not by me. I think literally everybody at the base turned out to see us. The crush around the P-38s was tremendous—our ground crews were practically breathing into the cockpits, and it was good to see Roy Silvers, my crew chief, and the familiar faces of many of the other men we had left behind in the U.S. The ground crews had crossed the continent by train and sailed from New York on the Queen Elizabeth, to arrive in Glasgow six days later. This was certainly a contrast to the journey of the P-38s. They could not believe the P-38s were in England at last and it was hard for us to realize the tortuous trip was at an end. We were glad to be with Americans again.

The 94th Fighter Squadron of the First Fighter Group settled down to business at once. We started training again. We learned aircraft recognition, studied maps of enemy territory, and were taught the British system about everything. An important new part of our study was air-sea rescue. We learned how to ditch our airplanes in the English Channel, and it was no easy matter. To crash land a plane in the water requires real technique, and sometimes when we didn't do a perfect job, the whole English Channel caved in on us and there was no doubt in my mind that the end had come. But sure enough it hadn't.

Air-sea rescue was man's best friend when you were hit flying over enemy territory and yet were able to make it out to the English Channel or the North Sea. The first thing we did was to tell our buddies that we were going to bail out of the plane or crash land in the water. If we were able to reach the Channel coast, we immediately used the special frequency on the radio, which signaled the air-sea rescue stations, and at the time we gave our call for help (often this was done by one of our friends because we were unable to do so), we also gave our approximate position. All this, of course, was done before the airplane was ditched, or before we were parachuted into the water. Then we waited, either floating in the water

94th Squadron pilots at Kirton - In - Lindsey, Lincolnshire, England - late July 1942. Standing (left - right) Jack Ilfrey, Sid Pennington (1), Jack Kille, Bob Neale, Norman "Cy" Wilden (3), Clarence Rimke (2), Glenn Hubbard, C.O., Jim Harman (2), George Sutcliffe (4), Robert Wilson (2). Kneeling (left - right) Earl Hille, Lewis Murdock, Donald Starbuck, Wesley Pringle (2), Clark Jennings, Newell Roberts, Dick McWherter (2), Clifford Molzan, Robert E. Williams. (1) Killed on Training Mission (2) Killed in Action (3) Prisoner of War (4) Wounded in Action

In front of the Officer's Mess at Kirton-In-Lindsey - late 1942; 94th Squadron pilots with the famous 303 Kosciusko Squadron. They were the wildest, flyingest, drinkingest bunch and taught us many tricks of the trade.

or sitting in the dinghy, a nice target for the enemy. Meanwhile, the air-rescue station had sent a plane to "fix" the exact position, and then a Coast Guard boat followed swiftly and we were on our way to base and food and safety.

The men in the Coast Guard cutters did a wonderful job in rescuing men right off enemy shores, under terrific gun fire, and engaged in fierce battles with German "E" boats, which were similar to our PT boats. They were fearless men and a constant kind of courage was required of them.

When British radios were installed in our airplanes, we had to learn radio procedure anew, and the hardest thing to absorb was the lingo. We could no longer fly on beams as we had done in the United States for the simple reason that the Germans would be able to pick up the same beams and intercept us at every turn.

While the British seemed glad to see us at Kirton-in-Lindsey, I thought their real attitude was, "Be nice to the Americans, regardless of the effort it costs us." I was mistaken. When you understand the mental makeup of the Britisher, you understand everything about him. And you admire him. He is a man in his own house and the head of his house.

We had nice quarters at this base, which was a permanent base like Randolph Field in the United States. Two men shared a room and we had to accustom ourselves again to the formalities of eating. The daily eating routine consisted of breakfast, mid-morning tea, lunch, afternoon tea, and dinner. At this time we were on RAF rations, which were supposed to be the best in England, and for breakfast we would have some kind of porridge or oatmeal (tasteless), a spoonful of sugar every other morning, with a skimmed milk substance. The porridge or oatmeal was usually accompanied by a couple of pieces of very dry bread-type sausage (hard to swallow), and once in a blue moon, an egg. You drove all this down with the unmitigated tea. And if hunger won out, you went back to the mess hall for the mid-morning tea. With the cup of tea, you get a slice of bread or a biscuit, which we call crackers.

Lunch was served around one o'clock in the afternoon, and the menu was invariably the same: soup of the dishwater variety, the inevitable brussels sprouts, and Yorkshire pudding. We always came back for the afternoon tea between four and five o'clock—an empty stomach will drive you pretty far—and ate the usual bread or biscuits and, on rare occasions, cakes or cookies. The English supper is a long affair and almost approaches a ceremonial. With nothing

Flag Pole at Kirton-in-Lindsey: RAF Flag; American Flag; Polish Flag.

CHAPTER 3: A New World and an Old World

Four Original Pilots in front of the Officers Club at Kirton-in-Lindsey. (Left to Right) Jim Harmon (Killed in Action), Cy Widen (POW), and Newell Roberts and Jack Ilfrey, who both became aces.

to do afterwards, the British officers lingered over their tea and tried to make conversation that would be of interest to the Americans. But it was hard to take an interest in what the Englishmen said. We were hungry—supper was a reproduction of lunch—and we missed salt and sugar and coffee. Later on when we moved to the South Channel coast, Ibsley near Bournemouth, for combat operations, we were grateful to get on American rations again, and if you don't think coffee can be clear out of this world into the next one, just stay off the beverage for a month.

Here at Kirton-in-Lindsey we had napkins, tablecloths, and a batman to wait on us. The batman is an enlisted man in the RAF, and he was a novelty to us at first. He woke us up in the morning, brought hot water for shaving, and the inevitable hot tea. He shined our shoes and pressed our pants, and he made us feel like millionaires, but he also made us a shade uncomfortable, too. We had been used to shining our own shoes, heating our own water, and doing everything for ourselves, and we felt the batman was a useless waste of manpower in wartime. He had no equivalent in the American army except for orderlies who served high-ranking officers, and here there was a well defined difference. Our orderly was regarded and treated as an individual, while the batman was just there, to serve, to move around unseen, not to be spoken to, shining shoes, and heating water.

My foot locker had arrived and little things, such as putting a few personal possessions around the room, helped your morale, and the many long talks I had with Roy Silvers helped, too. Roy had flown across the Atlantic in a transport and was to be my crew chief for months to come. A pilot and a crew chief get to be close, and it's a relationship you think of afterwards, with appreciation.

One night in the lounge one of the British officers started comparing our uniform with those of the British and the Poles. The British and the Poles had only two uniforms, and one was known as the full dress or the blouse, which they usually wore all the time, and the other was a battle jacket. Both uniforms were blue. The British officer expressed amazement at our combinations of dress. He pointed to the green shirts and the pink pants, and the pink shirts with the green pants. Then he called our attention to some of the men wearing khaki pants and green shirts, and there were still others with miscellaneous blouses, leather jackets, and green O.D. sweaters. Some of the American pilots wore G.I. shoes and a few had on officer's shoes.

We had a hard time trying to understand the Englishman when he started talking about clothes. He seemed to have the wearing apparel all mixed up. The gentleman in England wore suspenders instead of garters, braces instead of suspenders, vests instead of undershirts, pants instead of shorts, and trousers instead of pants.

Although it was mid-summer, it was too cool for us to wear our khaki clothes. Consequently, we dressed every day for Sunday, and it didn't seem to make any difference; but you could not explain our hodgepodge appearance to the Britisher. You had to be an American to understand.

The twenty-two American pilots (six had gone down on the Icecap) on this British base soon made friends with the famous 303rd Polish Squadron, which was stationed there for a brief rest while they were off combat operations. The Poles were a merry bunch of men. They could hold an immense amount of whiskey and once they were well-launched, they would start singing and fairly tear the roof off. Extremely rugged individuals, they were deadly enemies. I liked them.

When Poland fell, some of the men, a few of whom had fought in Spain with the Nationalists, had joined the French Air Force, while others went into the RAF. Eventually they all came into the RAF fold. For the most part, the Polish flyers were well-educated and had families back in Poland from whom they had not heard since the invasion of their country by the Germans. None of the pilots' names could be mentioned in newspaper dispatches describing their daring exploits because of brutal retaliation by the Germans to their families back home. Every Pole had no less than twelve or fourteen victories, and the commander of the squadron had even more.

The Poles showed us their combat films and helped us with the new fighter formations and fighter tactics we were trying out and developing. We had mock dogfights with them and learned a lot.

It was pretty much intensified training and while we were not green at flying, we were raw and unexposed when it came to the art of combat. We were among the first American fighter pilots in Europe, and later we were the first men home to teach combat after actual experience.

The British Girl Enters the Picture

I met the WAAF in my daily work. My first reaction was that she didn't use or take advantage of her femininity. And, second, I saw she was getting the job done. She ran the control towers, drove ambulances and gasoline trucks, cooked, washed, waited on tables, and did all kinds of dirty jobs. There was nothing glamorous about her work.

The British WAAF might have been ironically amused at her American sister who tripped daintily, dressed to the nines, down to the USO and gave two or three hours on the days she could spare the time, to entertaining the boys. The work at the USO made her feel patriotic, and it was not too tiring. Men were always around in abundance.

London Taxi - 1942

And there was the American debutante who gave ALL to the Red Cross a few hours each week, but who gave more attention to how she looked in her uniform than she did to the work at hand. Naturally, the debutante spent more time talking than she did working, and, naturally, she had to apply to the Rationing Board for extra gasoline. It was not possible for her to take a bus or a street car to Red Cross headquarters. No, I do not think the British girl would have been amused...

It's odd that a great number of American women can't do war work if they aren't sleekly dressed. Somehow they must have a uniform that is flattering and provoking. Somehow, even during wartime, the American male has got to be snared and kept aware of the fact that Betsy is still queen and homage must be paid. What would Betsy do should she ever be faced with total war?

The American women who made real contributions to the winning of the war were the women who worked in the factories, in the offices, the plants, served as nurses' aides in hospitals; they were the women who worked without pay in the Volunteer Coast Guard, the housewives who saved grease and paper and took good care of their families. There were the older women who did most of the work in the USOs and Stage Door Canteens, and there were the others who stood on the sidelines and mouthed patriotism.

The girl in British military service had no cosmetics, no silk stockings. The uniform did not do her justice and in comparison with the American girl, she had nothing to wear and nothing with which to make herself attractive. The WAAF didn't worry about black market nylons, and she wasn't concerned with what color matched what color. She was engaged in total war. She knew it. And she made the most of what she had. You never heard her complain. She wore her cotton stockings and blouse and shirt with dignity. And you respected her a hell of a lot.

I got to know several WAAFs well. They were nice girls, not so forward as the American girl, and were typical of the average English girl. You have heard a lot of stories about the morals of the women in Britain and, like all stories, they are somewhat exaggerated. England, like America, has all types and the average G.I. is usually looking for a certain kind of woman; and, thanks to his persistence; he nearly always finds what he wants. But what he finds should not be regarded as being representative. He doesn't have enough time for a complete survey of all classes, and he wouldn't be interested, anyway.

So the G.I. comes home and paints a sordid picture of the English girl and her home. In fact, according to the common story, her home is just a bawdy-house in disguise. The G.I. probably doesn't know it but such places can be found in the U.S.—there are American mothers and daughters who have an unusual understanding about these matters. And in both countries, these are isolated cases, not typical. If one even believed half of the stories one has heard in the U.S. about the Englishwoman, one would marvel they had any energy left for work. The Englishwomen worked hard and they worked long hours. Winning the war was their only thought, and all other things were incidental and secondary. It is not easy to be Madame DuBarry and a workhorse at the same time. Mother Nature, as a general rule, sees to that, barring, of course, exceptional individuals.

This was in 1942 and the influx of Americans had not yet come. We endeavored to be considerate of the British, trying to remember we were guests, and the men in the Air Corps did their best to behave like gentlemen toward the Englishwoman. Later, in 1944, this was not the case at all. The poor British were just outnumbered, and by that time the girls were so starved for male companionship that things were different but not radically so.

Take Pamela, for instance. She worked in the control tower, and if she had regular hours for working, I can't recall it as she always seemed to be on duty. If she wasn't in the control tower, then she was elsewhere. It was an event when she had a date. And a date with Pamela meant having a drink or two, dinner, dancing, talking about the war, international politics (imagine a junior leaguer indulging in such a discussion), and constantly wondering about England's future.

At twenty-two, Pamela had had enough experience and tragedy to last her a lifetime. Her home in London had been bombed and destroyed. Her parents had been killed. Her only brother was in the Royal Navy and she had not heard from him in months. But Pamela did not complain. She seemed to live only in the present and getting on with the war. Romance did not interest her particularly, and she was charitable of your pocketbook, and she did not become too personal. If she didn't care for you, you learned that quickly enough and still maintained friendly relations. The good old American technique was not applicable. The English girl was basically honest, and she was not a gold digger.

While we were at Kirton-in-Lindsey, the Dieppe raid came off. We did not participate, as we had just arrived and were still in training; but several American fighter squadrons, flying Spitfires, took part in the raid, with the Poles joining in.

We heard Dieppe was not just a commando raid. The idea back of the raid was for us to get a foothold in Fortress Europa. Unfortunately, the Germans knew all about the plan, well in advance of the scheduled date, and the whole thing was a tragic flop. In a way, one might say the British public was to blame for forcing the military authorities to undertake such a foolish venture. The people in Britain were clamoring at the time for a second front, with little or no knowledge of what it takes to make a second front possible.

CHAPTER 3: A New World and an Old World

Bicycles and Yankee Ingenuity

Almost all the British had bicycles, and if you wanted to get around, you had to have one. Transportation was difficult in England in 1942, and it was not a simple matter to hop into an automobile and go somewhere, as gasoline was severely rationed and motor vehicles were not plentiful. So one day six of us decided we were going into Scunthorpe to buy bicycles.

We had been told by everybody at the base that bicycles could not be obtained anywhere. Being Americans, this did not discourage us in the least. We knew we could find bicycles somewhere. We started out, hitchhiking and it wasn't long until a WAAF, who was driving a small English ambulance, picked us up. We told her what we were going into Scunthorpe for, and she said we were crazy. She said there were no bicycles to be bought anywhere in England at that time. And, naturally, we refused to believe her. Nevertheless, we accepted the WAAF's offer to pick us up on a certain corner in Scunthorpe an hour later, as she was returning to the base and it would save us a three-hour hike.

Within fifteen minutes after we had arrived in Scunthorpe we found a little shop that had six bicycles, and we felt we had vindicated America for Yankee ingenuity. It took us a little while to get used to the English bicycle as it does not have a coaster brake, but has hand-operated brakes on the handlebar. Also, the traffic is on the wrong side of the street, so everyone keeps left.

We had a wonderful time riding up and down the streets in Scunthorpe, disrupting traffic and having no knowledge at all of the regulations. The English stared at us, and I might add they did not seem to be amused. One striking difference was that the English ride their bicycles sedately and only as a matter of business, and we Americans ride our bicycles for the fun of it.

The WAAF could not believe her eyes when she stopped at the corner and saw us with six bicycles. At first she said the six of us could not ride in the ambulance, with the six bicycles, as it was against regulations to overload the ambulance. It was a simple matter to argue this objection down. Then she said the ambulance could not possibly get six men and six bicycles in it. While we were inclined to agree with the WAAF on this, each of us wanted to be sure that we got in the ambulance with our bicycles. After much pushing, squeezing, and scraping—heedless of paint being chipped off and spokes being bent—all six men and bicycles performed the feat, and we drove out of Scunthorpe, triumphantly waving good-bye to the large crowd that had gathered. All the way back to base the English girl kept expressing her amazement, first, at our locating the bicycles, and, second, at our being able to stow them away in the small ambulance, along with our anatomies.

When we were about three miles from the base we got out of the ambulance, so the excess weight would not subject the WAAF to criticism, and cycled on to base. Upon arrival, we had the time of our lives. We played tag, "Follow the Leader," rode through the hangars, and were the sensation of the day. You have to hand it to the British; the officers just looked at us and said nothing. They were polite and they weren't amused, and had the tables been turned, we Americans would have embarrassed them by laughing if they had cavorted with bicycles. But this was never the case with the British. They played the part of an excellent host, with great patience.

The next day we took some WAAFs into town for a few "mild and bitters", and, of course, we bicycled in and found this was strenuous work, with our extra passenger, over the narrow and winding English roads. The countryside was a continuous green—you passed from one little village to another and the stone houses with thatched roofs were a source of wonder to me. I kept thinking what happened to the thatched roofs when it rained, and it rains a lot in England. Since it was wartime, there were no road signs and getting lost was a major crisis, as the villagers seemed only familiar with the immediate vicinity in which they lived, and the next town a few miles down the road was often a foreign country to them.

We finally arrived at the pub, blowing and puffing for all we were worth, and we were surprised that the pub was a friendly place and that the natives were anxious to talk with us. I had my first Scotch and soda without ice that day (not bad), and also my first taste of English beer, just barely chilled (not good). It seemed funny to be in a pub. You'd heard about the public houses in England where the common people gathered but you never thought you'd be in one, and I didn't notice anything common about the people in the pub that afternoon. They looked like pretty regular people to me.

We fell to talking about various things and were told we were murdering the King's English. One of the WAAFs said we used a lot of funny expressions and we said, "Oh, no, we don't. You're the ones who use the funny expressions. For instance, you don't travel in an automobile. You travel in a motor car, and you call the top of the car a hood and the hood of a car is the bonnet. Instead of having a muffler on the car, you have a silencer. Your windshield is a windscreen, and whoever heard of having wings on a car? We call 'em fenders."

The WAAF said, "You're really the funny ones when you turn on the radio. We play our wireless set. We get our drugs at a chemist's and our cigarettes at a tobacconist's. And you get everything you need at a drug store," to which I replied, "That's true and we can also get some of our hardware at a drug store. We don't have to go to an ironmonger's. And what's more ridiculous than calling a roast a joint, and why don't you just say a rare steak instead of an underdone steak." The WAAF smiled and said she hadn't had a "rare" steak, and she hadn't seen a "roast" in so long that she'd forgotten what they tasted like.

The great day was coming. And it was hard to believe. All my life I had read about London. I had heard about it in grammar school and now I was going to actually see London town.

Bob Neale, Donald Starbuck, and I were lucky in getting a three-day pass, and, having heard a rumor that liquor was not plentiful in London, we took along a couple of quarts we had brought from the U.S., which we had carefully hidden in our P-38s.

The English train was entirely different from my conception of it. I expected to be uncomfortable, but I was quite comfortable. I thought the English would sit across from me in frozen silence, but I was a bit taken back when the Britishers who shared the compartment with us turned out to be friendly and full of questions. By the time we had finished one of the two fifths we had brought along, we were talking like mad, and the British reserve went out of the window. They liked our whiskey and seemed to regard our hospitality as a real treat.

When we came into Waterloo Station that night at eleven o'clock, all of us were old friends. And I mean friends in the sense that when we said good-bye we had a feeling of regret that we would not see them again. I stepped out of the train into night so black that I could not believe such blackness existed. I could see nothing. I don't know what I expected but the complete darkness was an anticlimax. We didn't even know where we wanted to go and we didn't know how to go even if we knew. And I didn't care. I just stood in the blackout and thought: Well, this is London.

London, 1942
Looking back now, it was a miracle that we found a cab, and what is more, we discovered a cabby who listened to our problem with sympathy. He became friendlier with each swig that we gave him out of our one remaining bottle and started thinking where we could spend the night. First, he said, we would try several of the well-known hotels.

We could see nothing as we drove through the streets and it was amazing how the cabby could drive perfectly through the black night, and, strangely enough, he did not drive too slowly. By degrees we became accustomed to the blackout and were able to make out that the curbs were painted white and that the blackout signals were still operating.

Our first stop was the Park Lane Hotel, and I was mortally impressed with its swankness, and especially its brightly lighted lobby, which was in sharp contrast to the darkness outside. Of course, the clerk was sorry, no rooms. Why didn't we try the Mount Royal? We did and it finally turned out that none of the hotels had any rooms. The cabby suggested, as a last resort, that we go by the new American Red Cross Club, and we were so tired by that time, it didn't matter. An exciting evening was out of the question now and the Red Cross Club sounded dull, good, and the end of everything for that evening—all at the same time.

And it was the American Red Cross that put us up for the night. We were grateful and a little ashamed of some of our thoughts. The Red Cross seemed to bring us a little nearer home. A part of America was here in this club and this thought, which never penetrated beyond your subconscious, gave you a deep, warm feeling; and even when the name America sounded strange and unreal, this feeling never deserted you when you were in American clubs or organizations.

Naturally, the next morning we had that good old tourist feeling. We had plenty of money, plenty of time, and plenty of curiosity, and we were almost bowled over when the woman at the desk in the club told us a car and a driver could be arranged for us; but she also warned it might cost us a great deal. I am afraid we were not impressed with her last remark, but we were later in no uncertain way. I believe we Americans, as a general rule, think of the cost afterwards—when it was a shade late. But that day we weren't concerned with expense—to hell with that. We were going to do London in a big way—but big.

We quickly learned from our driver that you don't talk about so many blocks in London. It's turnings. And we got an enormous kick out of traffic being on the wrong side of the street, and we remembered how we had to force ourselves to ride our bicycles on the left and think left, left, left. It was amazing to me how the narrow streets in London accommodated so much traffic, and once when our driver referred to something on the pavement, we automatically looked in the street, of course. It took us a few seconds to understand he was referring to the sidewalk. We would have been more confused if the driver hadn't been an excellent guide, with a talent for making things clear.

We drove down Sloane Street and saw the Victoria and Albert Museum, but we had no desire to see the museum even if it had been open, which it probably wasn't. Park Lane impressed us to some degree; however, the British millionaires' homes suffered a pretty poor comparison with those of the American millionaires. At the end of Park Lane was the beautiful Marble Arch.

We saw Savile Row where the finest suits in the world are made, and when we passed down Bond Street it looked like anything but the center of fashion. Burlington House was a gloomy looking affair, and I could well imagine what this royal academy was like inside. We drove through Hyde Park, entering by way of Rotten Row, and when we did not see any speakers mounted on soap boxes, we were disappointed. I suppose even in wartime we Americans expect the usual to go on.

Driving down Constitution brought us to Buckingham Palace and into The Mall and a glimpse of the palace gardens. Buckingham Palace was big and ugly, but not as large as we had thought it would be. Somehow we had pictured the king's house as an immense place, and its medium size let us down. The windows in the palace were boarded up and we looked hard to see if the king and queen were wandering around anywhere, but there was no sign of them.

All the buildings around Saint Paul's Cathedral had been badly hit, but the cathedral itself was hardly touched. It was interesting to note that the brick around the cathedral was piled in neat piles, awaiting the day when the job of repair could begin.

The Houses of Parliament and Big Ben looked just as they did in the movies, right on the edge of the Thames River, or on the River Thames, as the British would say. Big Ben was something to remember, and not too far away was Scotland Yard. We rode down Whitehall and saw the Cenotaph and looked at it for a long time. The inscription said simply, "The Glorious Dead."

Our last stop, just before lunch, was in Regent's Park. We didn't take in the zoo but we did a thorough job of Madame Tussaud's Exhibition. This was something that appealed to us, and it was a surprise to find the exhibition housed in a nice looking, modern building. The royal wax figures left me cold, with two exceptions: Queen Mary (if there was ever a really regal queen, she's it) and the Duchess of Kent (and she's a looker). I noticed the Duke and Duchess of Windsor were not in the royal group but elsewhere. Madame Tussaud's souvenir guide said that the Duchess of Windsor "claims to be of English stock." As most of us originally came over from England, I wondered if Madame Tussaud thought it was exclusive to be of English stock? Or was it just another sly attack on the Windsors?

CHAPTER 3: A New World and an Old World

I saw the effigy of Mae West in a costume worn by her in the picture, *I'm No Angel*. Mae looked good to me and it was nice to think I was looking at somebody from Hollywood, via Brooklyn. Katherine Hepburn, always one of my favorites, was there in a dress she had worn in The Little Minister, and looking vital, as usual.

The wax figures were remarkably lifelike. You felt this closeness to human beings upon entering the Chamber of Horrors. There was a man standing at the entrance to this hall, with his hand outstretched, and almost like a reflex action you had the desire to go up and shake hands, and then when you got right upon the man, the realization came that he was made of wax. There were benches in the Chamber of Horrors, with men sitting on them, and when you sat down you had the greatest urge to speak—with these figures looking right into your eyes, and, again, you realized just in time that they were effigies, but the whole thing gave you a feeling right out of this world into the next one.

The wax figure of William Godfrey Youngman fascinated me in a peculiar way, and also impressed me as unusually efficient. Not being content with just stabbing his girl friend, his mother, and two brothers to death, William proceeded to cut their throats. His hanging in 1860 was a great event, with 30,000 people witnessing the execution. Henri Desire Laundru was there, too, looking innocent of the fact that he had murdered ten mistresses and a boy. There was the Englishman, Patrick Mahon, who was hanged in 1924 for the murder of a Miss Kaye in a bungalow at Eastbourne. Patrick neatly disposed of the body by boiling pieces of it in a kettle. Yes, Madame Tussaud's was fascinating—and gruesome.

When we stopped for lunch, we insisted that the driver come in with us and he protested, saying, "This is most irregular, sir, most irregular." We just laughed at him and more or less dragged him into the Lyons Corner Tea House with us, and here we had our first experience with queue, that is, standing in line. At this time in England you didn't occupy a table all by yourself. The table was shared with as many people as chairs could be crowded around it. The menu that day was tea, sandwiches, and cakes. The cakes had no sugar in them but the tea was good, and I was beginning to like the national beverage. It was in Lyons I learned to ask the waiter for the "bill"—not for a check as we did in America.

Westminster Abbey was our first stop in the afternoon. When we had passed the Houses of Parliament that morning we decided there was not enough time to explore the Abbey, and it was the driver who suggested that we should see it, that we might not have another opportunity. And I am glad we saw the old Abbey. A deep, rich peace enveloped you within its ancient walls. England's famous slept there and the noise outside was completely shut out. We crossed London Bridge and all of us thought of the song we had sung in primary school.

The Tower of London took one back to the age when English history was being studied. London changed your moods constantly. Now the modern, now the present, then the old, and then the deep past.

We went back to Buckingham Palace for the changing of the guard, and we were in luck. The king was in residence, so we would see the Royal Horse Guards changing guard at the palace. With their tall plumed hats, red coats, white pants, and high boots, the Royal Horse Guards were really a sight. The horses were magnificent and were black, for the most part. I can only recall seeing one white horse, and it was a beauty. It might be a good idea to have a similar guard at the White House. It could serve as a reminder to all of us that the president is there, and, psychologically, it might add prestige. Americans do not exert themselves much to increase the prestige of our chief executive.

As we drove about London, I could not help noticing the various signs that were designed to appeal to the British for helping the war effort. This was certainly a distinct contrast to U.S. advertisements. For instance, one English sign read, "Feed the Guns with War Bonds and Help to End the War." There was no picture, just the words. The British did not seem to require dramatic presentations, written by advertising experts.

There was one thing I missed acutely in London: drug stores. There was no stopping in for a "coke" or ordering whatever one liked. And I also noticed a complete lack of public drinking fountains. I was beginning to notice that water was rationed carefully.

During the day we had bought tickets through a booking agent (not a box office) to see *No Orchids for Miss Blandish* at the Prince of Wales Theatre, and we said good-bye to our driver when he dropped us on Coventry Street in time for the 5:15 performance.

The program itself was interesting. It gave credit to Lydia Moss for lingerie and negligee and told us that the gowns worn by the women in the play were creations of Norman Hartnell, Queen Elizabeth's own designer. We were also told if an air raid warning was received, the audience would be informed; the announcer added that a warning did not mean a raid would take place, and assured those in the audience who desired to leave the theatre that they might do so, but that the performance would continue. The program gave out information that the theatre had been disinfected with Jeyes's Fluid. Smoking was permitted in this theatre and in all other London theatres, and the management even went so far as to make you more comfortable by providing ashtrays, which were strapped on the chairs.

Examining the program further, I found the action of *No Orchids for Miss Blandish* took place in Kansas City, Missouri, during the year 1933, and we had hoped to see a play with an English locale. The play was well-acted and the settings showed ingenuity, considering the scarcity of materials— and there was no air raid alarm. I did not experience any air raids in London during my stay there in 1942, but when I came back in 1944 it was quite different. I got acquainted with buzz bombs then.

When the play was over, we decided to see what was cooking in Piccadilly Circus. We had seen London for ten pounds, ten shillings, or approximately forty-six dollars, and without a price, we had observed what war can do to a country. It did not take much imagination to reconstruct the terrible damage wrought by the German bombers. The piled-up brick, skeleton buildings, and boarded-up windows were grim reminders. We enjoyed seeing London, but then, upon reflection, we didn't enjoy these remembrances. Certainly you were glad America hadn't been bombed, but sometimes you could not help wondering if a bombing would not have stopped some of the artificial flag-waving. We thought things like this. It was heartless. But there it was—and war has no heart. We in the service kept thinking Americans were hard to wake up. They were cocksure and pleased with themselves. The greatest nation on earth. Yes, that was true, but as the months rolled along there were reservations that popped up and stayed with us. And some of the reservations remain.

It was night when we reached Piccadilly Circus, and we meant to make the most of London's nightclub area. Without too much trouble, we located the Regent Palace Hotel, just off Piccadilly Circus, and made a beeline for one of its cocktail lounges. When we had fortified ourselves with Scotch and soda, we started making the rounds in earnest. The Ritz Bar didn't impress us much. We had been around in New York. The Britishers we ran into at the bars looked at us politely (they don't stare at people like we do), but left us to our own devices. The Scotch and soda had improved our morale considerably, and when we wound up at the Oddenino Dinner Club, the world was a damned good place in which to live. The war was something that didn't exist at the moment.

We had more drinks at the dinner club, the orchestra played "Tangerine," and once more we shocked the British: we asked the waitress to have a drink with us. Our invitation left her speechless for a minute, and when she had regained her composure she said, with a definite gleam in her eye, "Yes, I sure will, sir." International good fellowship had scored a point. She couldn't be uncooperative with the Americans.

We ordered pheasant and it was terrible. The potatoes didn't taste like the good old American spud, and it was but natural that we had the irrepressible tea. I struck up a conversation with a nice looking girl who was with her sister and brother-in-law, and they asked us to have drinks with them. So we invited the three to have drinks with us and eventually all the proper introductions were made. We talked about bowling and our English acquaintances referred to

My P-38F1 UN-O #417587 "Texas Terror" shortly after arriving in England.

a bowling alley as a skittle alley, and they called the installment plan (prior to this time I had thought the U.S. was the sole inventor of buying on time) the hire-purchase system. And when we fell to discussing automobiles, I had to ask questions. What was first speed? Low gear. What was an accumulator? A battery. A fender was a wing or a mudguard. A sedan was a saloon car. (This one nearly got me—I had conjured up a railroad car with a bar.) A multiple shop was a chain store. My calling a taxi stand a cab rank and a toilet a closet, to say nothing of referring to trucks as lorries. And I still think the most elegant name I learned in England was the English name for a freight car: goods wagon.

The 71st Fighter Squadron of the 1st Fighter Group at Ibsley; Commanding Officer Captain Rudi Rudell is standing just to the right of the guns.

CHAPTER 3: A New World and an Old World

My English friend proved to be a graceful dancer and much to my secret delight, the sister and brother-in-law had to leave, and when my dancing partner made no move to go with them, I knew my evening was not going to be a lonely one or an all-masculine affair.

Pretty soon two girls attached themselves to our party (or we attached ourselves to them—I don't remember), and we had a good party of six in full swing. The girls told us about clubs that were open all night and about clubs of which they were members. The clubs that remained open after the regular closing hours evaded the law by having members. Admittance to those clubs required membership, and unless you were a member you couldn't get on the wine list. A membership card read something like this:

Ilfrey, J. M.
The pleasure of your company is requested
at a private party being held at
11 P.M. tonight at
THE NUT HOUSE
94, Regent Street, London, W.1
Opposite Swallow Street.
IT IS ESSENTIAL TO BRING THIS INVITATION WITH YOU

For all outward purposes, the nightclubs were giving a private party and without an invitation or a membership card, you were simply out of luck. A membership card meant a bottle, and as time went on I was a member of several clubs. The bottle, however, might turn out to be American rye, American Scotch, or Scotch from Scotland—or almost anything else.

The first nightclub we went to had a good floor show and a first-rate orchestra. I noted, with keen satisfaction, that the floor shows were done in typical New York style. There were caricatures on the walls; however, upon retiring to the little boy's room, there were no Kilroys in evidence on the walls thereof—nevertheless, Smoe had made his appearance.

The owner of this nightclub was an old gal, somewhat of the grand dame type. She might have been of the Victorian age, with a few of the modern trappings added. She was happy to receive and entertain American servicemen (the private party idea being carried out to the letter). For this the guest merely dropped a good $50 in her lap for the spontaneous hospitality.

But it was a wonderful evening and when we left the club at 4:00 A.M. we faced the problem of finding a taxi. The underground had been closed since midnight, and after waiting an hour or so we got pretty desperate. So we made a taxi stop by literally making a human chain in the street out of three intoxicated second lieutenants. Once we were in the taxi my graceful dancing partner told me, in a suddenly firm voice, that she did not live far away, but when Peggy said good-night she asked me to come to see her and bring a friend.

The American Red Cross looked good to us when we drove up at 5:00 A.M. We had seen London night life. We were drunk and we were happy. There were times when you looked back and tried to think what night life in London was like. And you could only remember vaguely.

We slept until noon the next day when we finally dragged ourselves out of bed we felt like anything but more sight-seeing. But we were not persevering Americans for nothing. We had lunch at a fashionable restaurant and noticed that water was not served at all unless it was requested. We rode the English underground and found it nice and more comfortable than the New York subway. At first, riding the underground seemed to be a complicated system, but when you learned to follow the signs, it was a simple matter.

I 'phoned up Peggy and she invited the three of us out to her house for tea and to meet her family. We found the Thurlows very nice and hospitable, so kind, in fact, that we hated to leave. It was sorta like home. Peggy couldn't go out with us that night, so when we got back to the center of things, we decided we'd look in at a new Red Cross Club that had just opened. Officers were not usually permitted in the clubs but we were invited in because of the opening. And who should be there but Mrs. Roosevelt. We could scarcely believe our eyes. This was the first time I'd ever seen Eleanor and my first reaction was that all the photographs I'd seen of her were a grave injustice. She was far better looking than her pictures and she had a wonderfully radiant smile. When she spoke to you for a moment, you felt you were the only person she was interested in at that time, and that she had all day to talk. She impressed all of us with her sincere graciousness and made us know she was truly interested in our welfare and what we were doing. She was natural and simple, and you were completely at ease when you talked with her. Her critics may carp about her traveling around in wartime, but I'm here to say she did great good and a swell job.

Our first acquaintance with the girls, who were soon to be known as the Piccadilly "Commandos," were made that night. The technique of the Piccadilly "Commando" was something for her American sister to think about. There was a good reason why she was nicknamed "Commando." She wasn't afraid of anything—in pants. With the "Commandos" in tow, we made the bars in Piccadilly Circus.

I did not have to worry about a place to sleep that night.

Returning to base, after a leave, is always an anticlimax. At first you feel depressed, then gradually you become absorbed in the

The other side of my P-38F1 UN-O #417597 at Kirton-in-Lindsey. The name "The Mad Dash" was chosen by my Crew Chief. It was the name of a 1940s Comic Book character.

"In the Office," ready to go off to war.

routine, and the leave is pleasant to think about. It is also an inexhaustible subject for a week or two, and, naturally, our London experiences enlarged with each recital.

We had not seen the bomber pilots since we had flown over the Atlantic with them, as the bomber and fighter pilots were quartered at separate bases in England. So one day several of us flew over to see them and it was a happy reunion. The bomber pilots were just beginning to train again, learning new things, and I knew our time would be coming up soon.

We carried on a vigorous training program while at Kirton-in-Lindsey, and after a month we moved down on the South Coast near the resort town called Bournemouth. It was a beautiful town, modern, with pretty buildings, and clean. Bournemouth had not suffered much from enemy bombings and had nice hotels, dance pavilions, and bars. We were some of the first Americans in Bournemouth and, consequently, the British treated us like royalty. We enjoyed going to the picture shows there and had good meals in the hotel dining rooms. On the weekends we'd take a room at a hotel and it was an odd experience to find the price of a hotel room included breakfast. This meal was always the same: bread or fried toast, tea, and orange marmalade. I grew to loathe marmalade.

We started flying along the English Channel, getting the feel of things, and saw the French enemy coast. We were absorbing a little geography but these trips along the Channel were really quick dashes there and back to the base.

Then on Sept. 1, 1942, we went on our first fighter sweep. Our squadron, the 94th, with the other two squadrons of our group, 71st and 27th, led by Colonel Stone, penetrated fairly deep into enemy territory, sweeping the area for anything we might see. We were escorted by two Spitfire squadrons, making rendezvous with them at 24,000 feet over the English coast, then on to the French coast, making landfall south of the Somme River, in over a large area of northern France, and then back. We had been expecting the worst and the worst had not happened. Not an enemy plane was to be seen on our sweep, and when we landed at base we felt let-down while on the other hand, we were damned glad we hadn't engaged the Germans in combat.

Our American bombers started out on daylight raids over France, and we were their escorts. We were the first of the strategic air force going into Europe—we were guinea pigs and we knew it. But our accomplishments paved the way for the Mighty Eighth Air Force, which was to be operating against Germany within only a year. The British at first said it couldn't be done, that they had proved daylight raids were too costly, but we soon proved it could be done. Our technique of operating was different from that of the English. Instead of our bombers going out all over the sky, more or less individually, they stuck very close together, thus giving each other excellent protection. Then, too, the B-17s were heavily armed with ten to twelve .50-caliber machine guns, while any bomber the British flew was not half as heavily armed and had only .30-caliber guns, which were much less effective.

One of our first great raids was the bombing of the locomotive factories at Lille. Although it was pretty small and insignificant compared to some of the great raids on Berlin and Munich in '44, it was a big raid for September, '42, as we had only a skeleton of an air force when compared with that of two years later. Also, at this time we were not a match for the Germans. Despite the fact that we fighters did not encounter any opposition because we had become lost from the bombers, they were attacked by the famous Hermann Goering Yellow Nose Squadrons of Focke-Wulf 190s (JG 26). Several of our B-17s were lost, including Bennett and his crew, who had led me across the Atlantic to England.

Our bombers claimed so many victories that the British did not believe it, saying we couldn't do that type of thing, but we continued to do it and on a much larger scale. During the latter part of October, the British, in order to save face, made a daylight raid with Lancasters over Brest. They did not meet any enemy fighters. Nevertheless, daylight raids were still considered too dangerous by the British.

All during the month of September we went on diversionary sweeps and escorted bombers. We flew over Le Touquet, Hesdin, Abbeville, Neufchateaux, Dieppe, and other places, all the while expecting fierce opposition and never encountering it.

It was during this time that Eddie Rickenbacker came to visit us. He had been the commanding officer of our squadron in the last World War and had made the "Hat-in-the-Ring" insignia famous. Before our flight to England, Rick had come to see us in Long Beach, California, where we were serving as a part of the defense of the West Coast. He had wished us well at that time and now he was here to see if we were keeping up the tradition of his old squadron. We were doing our best and subsequent events helped us no end.

This was just the beginning of the bombing of Europe, and the Eighth Air Force was the pioneer. Altogether we made twelve missions into Occupied France during our stay in England. Then sometime during the last days of October we were called off combat operations. The ground crews were instructed to pack their clothes and the squadrons' equipment and in a few days they were loaded into trucks and driven away. We were all in the dark as to what was taking place. In a couple of days we pilots and planes flew over to a base near Land's End, in the extreme southwestern corner of the British Isles. Rumors went wild. We thought most likely we were

CHAPTER 3: A New World and an Old World

going to join the British Eighth Army in the Middle East, which had just started its offensive at El Alamein. But we could not imagine how we were going to fly there.

Along about this time we learned that Gen. Jimmy Doolittle had been in England for a month or so. We did not know why, but a wild rumor started floating around. With the development of our belly tanks for extra fuel, a couple of our Bolero Mission P-38 flights were in the air a full 8 hours. This was more than enough time and fuel to fly to Berlin and back. Was something up for us akin to Doolittle's Tokyo Raid?

Some of us might get to Berlin but felt sure as hell the Luftwaffe wouldn't let any of us return. We learned Gen. Doolittle was now C.O. 12th AF, preparing for Operation Torch - the invasion of North Africa.

Incident in Portugal
On the morning of November 8, the news broke over the radio that North Africa had just been invaded. Then we knew where we were going and felt sure that now we would get into plenty of action. Col. John N. Stone, our group commander, called us all into the briefing room on the night of the eighth, and told us where we were going and what we were going to do. He said our squadrons were to fly nonstop from England to Oran some 1,500 miles away, with a possible emergency stop at Gibraltar, 1,200 miles away. This was to be a very long nonstop flight for a P-38. Charts and maps were brought out and we spent several hours in feverish study, with high-ranking American and British officers giving instructions on every detail. Up to this time, Algiers, Casablanca, and Oran had just been names to us. A new world awaited us.

The ground crews had squeezed every ounce of gasoline they could get into the tanks, including the external drop tanks. We were ready for our nonstop flight to Oran, and suddenly I was sorry to leave England. Somehow it was home. In England they knew a war was going on and in America they had not waked up yet. The letters from your family and your friends told you that.

It was November 9, 1942, and I was about to embark on an unknown future. The invasion of North Africa had just begun the day before and I knew we were going to be something besides guinea pigs. Sometimes a few guinea pigs survive.

Our instructions sounded simple enough when we had heard them in the briefing room the night before. We were to fly in groups of eight, with a B-26 bomber leading us (319th Bomb Group). The route kept hammering in my brain: fly across the Bay of Biscay, hit the Spanish coast, fly down the Spanish and Portuguese coast, turn left, and go through the Straits of Gibraltar. Hit the Spanish Moroccan coast and fly around this coast into French Morocco and then into Oran.

Colonel Stone had told us at briefing that it was uncertain as to where the enemy might be on our route, and we were cautioned to be exceptionally alert and warned again and again that Gibraltar should be our first emergency stop.

I learned much later that some of the American Spitfire groups and P-40 groups had flown off carriers at Casablanca, but the P-38s were the first to fly down to Africa. It looked pretty simple but it turned out otherwise.

As I turned away from the base at Land's End, I had a true feeling of "This is it." We knew things were rugged in North Africa, and we knew the chance of survival was going to be hard. But you didn't think about death—you only thought of living. And you thought of a lot of other things, too. I wondered what my mother was doing in Houston and by now it was difficult to picture in my mind's eye what my mother looked like. When you're off at war,

Bob Neale at Kirton-in-Lindsey. General Monk Hunter made him take off the name.

everything becomes abstract. You don't have vivid mental pictures of things back home.

It was now seven o'clock in the morning and I was beginning to feel a little tired. We had left England around 6:30, just as daylight was breaking, and I had been up since 2:00 A.M. That morning in England had been cool and damp and misty.

Strict radio silence was being maintained across the Bay of Biscay, and we were flying low—just above the wave tops so we could not be detected by the enemy. We saw no German planes but several days later some long-range German fighters came out and shot down a few of our planes going to North Africa.

This was a bigger adventure than flying over the Atlantic. We felt this time we were going to get into real combat and later events proved to be more than correct in this respect. Of course, the old American custom of joking and laughing it off prevailed. Everything was so new to us—England had seemed quite different from the United States, and yet we were to find that the British Isles were very much like our own country when compared with other countries we saw.

There was a low overcast that morning. Good weather had been predicted all the way to Oran, but I felt an uneasiness I was unable to analyze. It's good we didn't know the higher-ups had prophesied only 50 percent of us would make the trip to Oran, and as the minutes passed the flight was proving not to be quite as difficult as we thought it would be. It had been made plain at briefing we were not to land at Gibraltar unless it was a real emergency, as The Rock was jammed tight with personnel.

Suddenly I felt a slight jolt and by the time I realized what had happened my right engine went out. One of my long-range belly tanks containing 150 gallons of gasoline had fallen off. Automatically, I switched to another tank and the right engine caught on again. But one fact was crystal clear. I had lost 150 gallons of gasoline.

I was still flying low. And then I saw Tony Syroi coming close to me and in his hand he was waving a map for me to see. In large letters, he had printed, ONE BELLY TANK. I nodded that I understood. He couldn't tell me over the radio I had lost a belly tank. Tony was an Italian and we had often joked about the time we would fight his relatives. I thought of our jokes again fleetingly and then my mind got really busy.

I didn't want to go back to England. I wanted to stay with my outfit. I got out my maps and charts and after a few quick mental calculations decided I had enough gasoline to get me as far as Gibraltar and dismissed all thought of turning back. I was not going to miss out on the operations in Africa and I was not going to be separated from the gang. And, being honest, I have to say I wasn't going to miss the big adventure ahead—Africa. Maybe I was thinking of lions and tigers. I don't know.

We kept on flying and when the B-26, which was leading us, dodged a thunderhead by turning west, I had the feeling we were getting off the course. I flew for another hour, and I began to get a little worried. After another hour passed I began to get alarmed. My gas was running low as we had used a great deal of fuel in dodging thunderheads. And still no coast in sight. We were pretty far out to sea. I knew that much and I knew we were flying in a southwesterly direction. I decided to leave the group, as my gas wouldn't last much longer.

I turned south eastward and hoped to hell I would run into the Spanish or Portuguese coast. The clouds were dispersing and when the sun came out I hoped I would be able to see the coast. And in a few minutes I saw it when I was flying at an altitude of about 8,000 or 10,000 feet. Again I got out my maps and saw that I was close to a point on the coast which was marked the Spanish-Portuguese border. I then flew parallel to the coast and after a short time realized I would never make it to Gibraltar. My gasoline was almost gone.

There are no words to describe the feeling you have when you are 8,000 to 10,000 feet up in the air and know your gasoline is going to be exhausted soon. The best description I can give is that you have a kind of paralysis with part of your mind still functioning between what to do next and hoping for something you know isn't going to come true. One minute I decided to bail out. The next minute I thought I'd crash land on the coast. While I was still wavering, I came to the mouth of the Tagus River, which, according to my map, ran 20 or 30 miles into Lisbon. We had been poorly briefed about what to do if we were forced down in Portugal or Spain. I vaguely remembered someone saying the Portuguese were friendlier than the Spaniards and might be bribed to get you out of the country. I knew, too, that it was the duty of every pilot forced down in enemy or neutral territory to destroy his plane and equipment. Still not knowing definitely what I would do or should do, I turned inland and headed toward Lisbon.

And presently I saw a beautiful airdrome lying just outside the city of Lisbon—long beautiful runways and big administration buildings. Everything looked inviting and seemed to beckon a welcome, and, without another thought, I put my wheels down, circled the airdrome, and landed.

When I had completed my landing roll, I saw six men, mounted on horseback, galloping out to meet me. The horsemen looked like something out of a picture book. Big, plumed hats, sabers, pistols, and multi-colored trousers, and for a split second I thought of the changing of the guard at Buckingham Palace. Gesturing wildly, the men motioned for me to taxi my plane toward a building which turned out to be the administration building, and, meanwhile, I was hurriedly tearing up maps, papers, and throwing them to the wind, and with more frantic gestures, the guards told me to stop on the apron just in front of the building.

When I killed my engines I looked up and saw people coming from every direction toward my plane. Some of the people in the crowd gave me the "V" for victory sign, but most of them just stared, and by this time the horsemen had surrounded my plane.

I stepped out of the cockpit and looked down at the crowd and I felt like a stranger to myself. It was almost impossible to believe I was in Portugal, about to become an internee. When I inquired if anyone spoke English, a young fellow who looked sort of ex officio came up and said he did. As I remember the conversation, it went something like this:

"You are an American, yes?"

"I certainly am an American." (Why I said certainly I don't know—unless it was subconscious pride coming to the front.)

CHAPTER 3: A New World and an Old World

The Portuguese smiled and said: "Yes, I thought so. I see the star on your airplane. It is the first American warship that I have seen." (A distinction of sorts here—the first P-38 to be forced down in Portugal.) Then he added, still smiling: "In trouble?"

My reply was serious enough: "Yes, I am in trouble. I need some gasoline. Is it possible for me to get any?"

The fellow gave a short laugh. "Come with me and I will take you inside." As I walked away I glanced back and everyone was staring at me and at my plane in amazement. I felt a sudden alarm about my airplane and I asked the Portuguese official if anyone would bother the plane and he spoke to one of the guards who commanded the people to stay away from the P-38.

As I started in the administration building the first thing to strike me in the face was to see some of our American Douglas DC-3s with big German swastikas on them. From all appearances, they were airliners, and when I got inside the building I saw the German pilots of these airliners. It made me furious to see that they had our planes, but of course the planes had probably been bought before the war.

I was taken into the restaurant at once and given cake and coffee. The coffee was terrible and the cake even worse. By this time more Portuguese officials had arrived and I was being asked my name, home address, and questions about everything under the sun. One of the officials, who spoke excellent English, told me the American Legation had been notified. I wondered if this could mean anything and decided it didn't—at least for the time being. I heard a commotion outside and looked out just in time to see a big car skidding to an abrupt stop and some excited Portuguese pouring out. They made it into the restaurant in no time flat. And more questions. Where was I going? I said I could not tell them. Where did I come from? And again I refused to answer.

I could see the Portuguese officials did not like my attitude. They had expected a little information and had received none. No doubt any information received from me that day would have been in the possession of the Germans by night.

Then a new tack was tried. They had seen some American planes passing over earlier in the day. Had I done any fighting against the Germans? I neither denied or affirmed this. One of the officials made the comment that since I was flying a warship and was a fighter pilot, I must have fought the Germans, and all this time the German pilots were gathered around me and listening intently. Their faces were grim and it was hard to believe one was in a neutral country in such a tense atmosphere. It seemed definitely pro-German and anything but neutral. You didn't have to be psychic to feel hatred coming from the officials. Their politeness was only surface and not very deep surface at that. The people outside had not seemed at all antagonistic, and the contrast with the officials was a curious one.

The questioning must have gone on for an hour or more. The Germans stood rooted. They did not move once. At first I thought I had been the one who had stood still. I seemed to be in a trance at times—I could hardly realize where I was—but one thought crowded out all others: I must not say anything. I must not say one word that would be a clue.

One of the Portuguese officials, who had been in the background, stepped up and told me in cool, crisp English it was the policy of Portugal, being a neutral country (I had the greatest urge to laugh at this), to intern all foreign pilots and their planes. That was a shock and the full realization really hit me. If I ever felt alone, it was at that moment. My friends had gone on. I would not see them for a long time. I was out of the war and the adventure had come to an end. And my airplane would be taken away. That hurt. A plane is as close to a pilot's heart as a ship is to a sailor. When your plane goes, a part of you goes, too. I had had no desire to fight a war. My country needed help and that was all I knew. Now here I was in Portugal, about to be interned, cut off completely. I'd never get any mail. And I'd never know what was going on.

I was introduced to a Portuguese pilot and he asked me if I would show him something about the P-38. He said he had never seen one before and that he was amazed at its looks. He told me the Portuguese air force was made up mainly of interned German, British, and French planes, and he repeated my airplane was the first American warship he had seen, that he was going to take the plane and fly it over to a military airfield.

We walked outside and it seemed to me there were thousands of people looking at me. I forgot to be self-conscious. I knew people were looking at me, and I saw people and that was all. Something had happened to my consciousness. I was floating along, coming out of a dream that was real and then it wasn't.

The Portuguese pilot asked me what type of fuel the P-38 used, and I told him 100 octane gasoline. He said they had no 100 octane and would 85 octane gasoline do? I thought for a moment before answering and finally told him yes. And when the Portuguese asked me to show him the various mechanisms of the P-38, I saw nothing wrong with that, as the plane had to be taken off the commercial field and flown to a military base. The mechanic finished gassing up the plane as I climbed into the cockpit. Almost everything had been removed. My Mae West was gone and my parachute was gone. I had stuffed my billfold, which contained my A.G.O., or identification card, and overnight bag behind the seat and these had also been discovered and removed. There were a few maps, however, still in the cockpit, which had been overlooked.

The Portuguese aviator sat on the wing while I explained the various uses of the switches that go into the operation of a P-38, and all the time I was talking with the foreign pilot, my conscience kept bothering me. I kept thinking I should have destroyed my plane and I had a feeling of disloyalty because we had been told to destroy our plane in the event we were forced to land. I glanced at the hundreds of people (and this time I could see clearly there were not thousands) standing around and I looked at the guards surrounding the airplane, and my emotions were really mixed-up. Some of the officials were still in evidence, jabbering among themselves, and as yet no one had put in an appearance from the American Legation. I was one forlorn pilot.

Suddenly, I heard a familiar, faint sound, and then a louder noise, and I looked up and saw a lone P-38. It was in trouble and making preparations to land. The six guards on horseback dashed off and people started running towards the end of the ramp to watch

Jim Harmon's P-38F1 at a Portuguese air base. The aircraft now bearing Portuguese Air Force markings.

the landing. The P-38 was putting its wheels down and was landing on one engine.

I held my breath and all of a sudden it struck me. "Ilfrey, what the hell are you waiting on?" I threw on all the switches and while I was doing this, the Portuguese pilot realized what was about to take place and he tried to reach inside the cockpit and turn off some of the switches. But lightning had hit, and I had already turned over my left propeller and the engine started; and the pilot, who was sitting on the left wing, lost his hat when the propeller created a terrific wind, which sent what was left of the crowd scurrying away. When the pilot started trying to get a better grip on the plane, I started my right engine and threw on lots of power, creating a bigger wind than ever and managed to keep the airplane still. My idea was to blow the pilot off the wing, which I did in just another second or two, and when I looked back—after the Portuguese had cleared the plane—I saw the officials holding on to their hats while many others were chasing their headgear, and, believe me, there were plenty of Portuguese hats flying in the air. I threw the canopy shut, gave the plane full power, and without looking back went straight across the field, disregarding runways and everything else in my path.

As I was leaving the field, I saw the identification mark on the P-38, which had just landed. The plane belonged to Jim Harman, a member of my squadron. Beyond this, I didn't think. I was too busy rolling up the windows and doing other things.

Once I was in the air the full realization of the harrowing take-off fairly shook me. I had no parachute, no helmet, and most of my belongings were gone. But I gave no further thought to these things and set an estimated course for Gibraltar, which would take me across Portugal and Spain. I just hoped they had put in enough gasoline for the 400-mile trip.

I was flying in bright sunlight, which was certainly a contrast to the mugginess in England, and the Portuguese villages below me looked pretty and picturesque. The conscience still pursued me, however, and although I knew I had violated international law in wartime and was getting to Gibraltar the quickest and safest way, I did not realize to what extent or degree I had broken the law.

The Rock was like a beacon as I approached Gibraltar, and I had no trouble in finding the airdrome or receiving landing signals. On my way to the operations office I met several other boys in my squadron who had been forced to stop on their way to Oran, and, of course, I had to explain where I had been and how I had got out of Portugal, and my mates expressed amazement and almost disbelief. And when I repeated the story of my flight from Portugal to the operations officer, he, too, looked disbelieving and hinted of complications.

It wasn't long before I was taken in to see Colonel Willis, who was in charge of the American operations at Gibraltar and who had been a member of the Lafayette Escadrille in the last war, and when I had told my story once more, to say that he was mad is saying

CHAPTER 3: A New World and an Old World

nothing at all. He was blind, furious, raging mad. He gave it to me up one side and down the other. Half the time he was incoherent—so was I—and all I remember was that he kept storming about international complications, why didn't I use my brain, why didn't I think, why didn't I destroy my plane, etc., etc., etc.

After about forty-five minutes of this tongue-lashing, the colonel broke out into a big, healthy laugh and said it was a good trick after all. In fact, he almost congratulated me on getting out of Portugal. Finally, he dismissed me and I joined my squadron mates in the officers' club at the other end of the Rock, and later on in the evening—after I had celebrated a little too much—Colonel Willis sent for me again. The captain who came for me decided I was in no condition to see the colonel, and certainly I was in no condition to discuss such a grave problem as international complications. When the captain left he warned me to be at the colonel's office at nine o'clock sharp the next morning.

My good friends who had celebrated with me didn't wake me up until ten o'clock, and when I finally got into the colonel's office he was madder than ever and not only repeated the previous day's performance but really gave me the works. I stood there shaking, from the dressing down and also from the hangover. My brain wouldn't function. I couldn't have thought of anything to say even if the colonel had stopped for a moment. He commented acidly on my unshaven appearance, said my airplane had been locked up, and that he had a good mind to lock me up, too. At last I mustered up enough courage and energy to tell him I hoped he didn't really expect me to go back to Portugal, that surely Colonel Stone, the C.O. of my group, would be able to figure out something. With that Colonel Willis gave me a slightly frozen smile and dismissed me, and despite his noncommittal air, the slight smile gave me hope. I couldn't believe Colonel Willis would send me back to Portugal, Washington notwithstanding, and I knew it wouldn't be long before Washington would be in the picture. I had a great faith in the army's ability to circumvent officialdom.

I felt so optimistic that I relaxed and proceeded to look Gibraltar over thoroughly. The weather was warm, even at this time of year, and I went swimming, toured the Rock in a jeep, and walked through its many tunnels. It was amazing to see the compactness and the efficiency of the offices in the Rock.

The city of Gibraltar is built just like a fortress, and only grim business went on here. There were many boats in the harbor, and the airstrip was a one-way affair on a flat spot behind the Rock. Thirty feet on the other side of the airstrip was the Spanish border, and I was told the Spaniards would shoot you down if you flew over Spanish territory. It gave you a curious feeling to see German observers with their telescopes watching everything that went on in the harbor and on the airstrip.

Late that afternoon I was summoned to the colonel's office again. He told me briefly that the Portuguese Government had notified Washington and that he was under instructions from the War Department to send me and my plane back to Portugal to be interned. I just stood there stunned, refusing to believe what I had heard. I must have looked pretty pathetic because the colonel got up and came around to me, gave me a friendly pat on the shoulder, and said not to worry, and I was again dismissed.

Hope was soaring so high that I joined my buddies and we met a Spanish boy who had offered to take us on a little sightseeing expedition into Spain. We were all dressed in khaki clothes and looked exactly like civilians. The Spaniard took us in his little boat across the harbor to Algeciras and much to my surprise, we found a nightclub doing a thriving business. The liquor was plentiful but not very good. We watched the dancers and thought them fair. The Spanish women seemed to put everything they had into their dancing, but there it stopped as far as I was concerned. They didn't have much to appeal to the American male.

The next morning rumor reached me that Colonel Willis had cabled to Washington that the "dumb John" pilot who had landed at Lisbon and later at Gibraltar had been sent to join his outfit in North Africa. He was sorry Washington's instructions had been received too late. I never saw the colonel again but I've thought of him a thousand times with a gratefulness that will not tarnish with time.

I left that day for Oran, with high hopes and in high spirits, but was soon to wish I had never heard of North Africa.

A Quote from *My Three years With Eisenhower, The Personal Diary of Captain Harry C. Butcher, USNR, Naval Aide to General Eisenhower 1942-1945*. Simon and Schuster, New York: 1946

"As if Ike didn't have enough worries - one of our American pilots flying a P-38 from UK to Gib landed at Lisbon for gas, having lost one spare belly tank, was told he was thereby interned. Told the Airdrome official he wanted to clear his superchargers or something, got back in plane, started motors, and dashed away, leaving his jacket with identification papers. Fearful of a diplomatic upset for thus flouting Portugal, and of indicating a "mightier than thou" attitude, Ike had Gruenther radio our Ambassador at Lisbon the story and to be prepared to answer questions frankly. Consideration would be given to return the lad and plane for internment."

A Quote from *I Could Never Be So Lucky Again*, an autobiography by Gen. James H. Doolittle with Carroll V. Glines. Schiffer Military Books, PA:1991.

"Two of my principal worries were the concentration of aircraft on Gibraltar and the long flight down from the U.K. in the season of bad weather.

Two P-38s landed in Portugal. One took off under a ruse and the other is interned."

4

NORTH AFRICA

Tafaroui was fifteen miles out of Oran and not a place where you'd plan a honeymoon. Everything was fouled-up and everybody was confused, but it gave me a good feeling to be back with my squadron, and I was brought up to date. Bob Neale, one of my buddies, had missed Oran on his way down, run out of gasoline between Oran and Algiers, crash landed, and spent several days with the French. One of the boys in another squadron had been shot down by the Spaniards when he had flown too close to Spanish Morocco. Our ground troops had come by boat from Southampton and had taken part in the invasion of North Africa but were not yet at the base in Tafaroui.

Everyone was anxious to know what had happened to me and I got pretty tired of telling about my escape from Portugal. In fact, I preferred not to think about it; there was always the chance that the State Department might outwit the army and I'd be back in Portugal, properly interned—too bleak a thought to consider.

The sequel to the Portugal story is that Jim Harman, who had landed behind me in Lisbon, joined our outfit about four months later in North Africa, and he had developed an anger at me which was reminiscent of the colonel at Gibraltar. It seemed that one of Jim's engines had started acting up and he got the same idea about landing in Portugal that I did. He had seen a P-38 take off as he was landing and thought to himself, *It looks simple, I'll just get some work done on my engine and be on my way.*

But it turned out differently. The minute he stopped his plane and chopped his engines, the Portuguese grabbed him by the back of the neck and Jim never saw his P-38 again. He was thrown in the local jail for a few days and later sent to an internment camp on the Spanish-Portuguese border. He said I was to blame for the rough treatment he received, and I felt a little guilty at first and then was consoled when I remembered the first law of nature. It was nearing the end of the third month of his confinement that the American Legation supplied Jim with civilian clothes and spirited him out of the country on a Dutch liner. He told me a few days after he landed in Lisbon six P-39s were forced down, interned, and thanks to the good old American Legation, all six men got back to their organizations eventually.

I was in a sad way. The Portuguese had relieved me of all my clothes. My foot locker had not arrived from England and clothes didn't exist in North Africa. But if I had no clothes, except those on my back, I did have a few delicacies in the food line. Arabs came to the airdrome selling figs, oranges, eggs, and walnuts. Eggs had been scarce in England and now something happened to your taste buds when the egg slid down, and I may as well say ever since I've had

Me sitting on a derelict Vichy French Dewotine 520 fighter at Maison Blanche airfield.

Vichy Dewotine 520

CHAPTER 4: North Africa

a great reverence for the egg. There were dates, too, of which you quickly tired. Also, you got a little tired of the dates making excessive demands on nature and having to go out on the desert and squat until your knees felt like inanimate objects. And another thing: the desert was about as private as Broadway and Forty-second Street. The natives stared and military personnel laughed. There are times when one likes solitude and a good magazine to read.

The Arabs sold their products reasonably in the beginning but it wasn't too long until they discovered one of our national weaknesses, and then came inflated prices and much bartering and trading.

The sleeping quarters at Tafaroui could not be compared in any way at all with accommodations at the Ritz-Carlton and especially the toilet facilities. We pilots slept on the floor in a building that was just on the verge of collapsing. Sleeping on a bare floor may relax the nervous system, but it doesn't add any prestige to the anatomy. An invisible welcome sign hung on the door of our shack for all insects who cared to come and share the doubtful pleasure of their company with us. When our bedrolls finally arrived from England, we knew seventh heaven had arrived.

One afternoon a gang of us hitchhiked into Oran, and I don't know quite what we expected to find but we were surprised to see the modern buildings, which were, for the most part, white - and dirty. There were plenty of Arab women on the streets, dressed in veils and sheets (this is the most descriptive word I can think of), and I don't think the sheets which covered their bodies had been taken off and washed in years. The women were indescribably filthy and it was something of a shock to see them going barefoot. Somehow bare feet were not in the picture. And there were Frenchmen wandering around and French girls looking chic. The Frenchwoman seems to be able to maintain a certain amount of style, regardless of where she is and what is going on.

The little Arabs attracted our attention the most. They had unusually serious faces and were pretty dirty children. They would follow us up one street and down another, crying, "Cigarette por

Lewis Murdock sitting in front of his tent covered foxhole, writing letters. Youks-Les-Bains, Algeria; November 1942.

papa!" Actually, if you gave the children a cigarette it was not for "papa," but would probably be sold later or smoked by the children themselves. We naturally felt sorry for these kids and gave them all cigarettes, and it was a heartening sight to see their little faces beam with several layers of dirt on top.

That evening we had a very good dinner at the Hotel Continental for 100 francs or 75 cents. When we finished eating dinner we made a straight path for the bar and rooted ourselves in chairs until closing time. We tried champagne, which was good, cognac, and all kinds of liqueurs—in fact, we ran the gamut of the wine list—and we bought drinks for the French girls who were in the bar. The girls couldn't speak English, and we couldn't parlez-vous, but we soon learned what "voulez vous coucher avec moi" meant, and the sign language held no barriers. The girls were smartly dressed and wore their hair in big pompadour hairdos. On our way back to the old French airdrome that night, we decided the French had something on the ball—at least the female component.

Living in the desert. 94th Squadron clerk and Ground Officer eating in their "dining hall." Flight line can be seen in the background. Youks-Les-Bains, Algeria; November 1942.

Lt. Bob Wilson by his tent. Pinned to the outside of his tent were a new set of Kansas license plates that followed him through the mail. Wesley Pringle on the left; Clarence Rimke on the right. All three of these men were killed in action.

41

We stayed at Tafaroui for a few days longer and then flew several hundred miles on to Maison Blanche, an airdrome not far from Algiers. We didn't know what was going to happen, but we did know that everything was being moved to Algiers.

The airfield near Algiers was once held by the German Luftwaffe. Real estate changed hands frequently during the North African Campaign. We inspected some derelict German aircraft at the base but were not impressed with the Junkers Ju-88 and Ju-52 that we examined. We thought our own aircraft were superior in every way.

The Initiation - York's Les Bains
Eight of us got up early the following morning, long before daylight, and were on our way to our first real combat assignment in North Africa: to ground strafe the airdrome at Gabes shortly after daylight. And we were initiated to concentrated firing that morning—being fired at. In the process of dodging ground fire, the eight of us got pretty well separated and when I turned up with Newell Roberts we proceeded to fly back across a small space of desert to the mountains and over to base. About halfway home, Roberts saw two planes in the distance, going the opposite direction from us.

He said to me over the radio, "Jack, they don't look familiar. Let's go see what they are." As we turned toward the planes we recognized them as enemy because they had gunned their engines, causing black smoke to come from the exhaust, and when we approached closer we could see the airplanes were ME-110s—German two-engine bombers. I said to Roberts, "Let's go after 'em." And his voice was shaking with excitement when he replied: "Roger, I'll take the one on the right and you take the one on the left."

These were the first German planes we had seen in the air and it was hard to realize we were going in to shoot them down. We closed in behind them and I must have opened up at 5,000 yards distance—about five times too far behind for bullets to be effective. I pulled in closer, got the German bomber squarely in my sight and let go again. This time the bullets took effect. About this time I saw something red coming out of the back of the German's plane and I realized later the "something red" was the rear gunner in the ME-110 firing tracer bullets at me!

Me in front of an abandoned Messerschmitt ME-110C-2 at Youks-Les-Bains, Algeria.

Ancient Roman baths, Youks-Les-Bains, Algeria 1942. (Credit - Ken Sumney)

Meanwhile Roberts had successfully hit the other enemy plane and it had crashed and exploded. The plane I had shot down had hit the ground and crash landed. Two of the crew of three jumped out and it was a funny sight to see the two Germans running on the ground, as it was flat desert and there was no place to hide or to run. While I circled around to set the downed bomber on fire with my cannon shells, Roberts started teasing the two Germans who were running by diving down low and giving them a few squirts from his machine guns. He was not actually trying to hurt them, just scaring hell out of them.

We had made our first real contact with the enemy that day in North Africa. Roberts and I were the first two pilots in the outfit to get an enemy plane. We had scored a victory...

In the meantime, things were happening to some of the other pilots. Sutcliffe and Widen got lost on the way back to the base and had landed together in a field. After studying their maps, with some help from the Arabs, they discovered they were not too far from the airdrome, so they drained the gasoline out of Widen's airplane into Sutcliffe's ship, which enabled Sutcliffe to fly back to base, fill his tanks with gas, and go back to the rescue of Widen. It was some job transferring gasoline from one plane to another, with only the aid of a five-gallon can, and when Sutcliffe and Widen returned to base, both of them looked beat-out.

We thought we had lost McWherter for sure. No report had come from him all day long but towards dusk he came rolling in, with a tale to tell. He, too, had got lost on the way back and had landed near an Arab village. The Arab chieftain had taken him in, fed him, and secured fifty gallons of automobile gasoline from a nearby French garrison. Of course, the automobile gasoline damaged McWherter's engines, but the important thing was that he returned safely.

Finally, we were all accounted for and our morale was still high. We now considered ourselves seasoned fighter pilots, although we had much yet to learn, it looked like we were well on the road to reestablishing the tradition of the old Hat-in-the Ring Squadron.

CHAPTER 4: North Africa

Major Sherry, our group intelligence officer, had been a member of Eddie Rickenbacker's World War I organization and prior to enlisting in the Second World War, had been a banker in Syracuse, New York. Sherry had shot us a lot of bull about the great daring and heroism of the pilots in Eddie's old squadron, but it was hard for us to reconcile what he told us with the aircraft we knew in 1942. The planes that Rickenbacker and Sherry flew in 1918 were not much better than the primary planes in which we first learned to fly. Now, instead of speeds of 130 to 150 miles per hour, our P-38s were doing a 280 to 300 miles an hour. Sherry had done his job O.K. in the First World War, with several victories to his credit, and now he was living in the same mud with us, very much interested in our welfare, and he had plenty on the ball. He knew what it was all about and he could give you the right answers. He wore a little mustache and was balding. He was personality plus.

For the first few weeks we were low on food and water. We had just enough water to brush our teeth with but none for washing the face or other parts of the body. Whenever we shaved, and it wasn't too often, we heated the water in our tin helmets, and now and then we managed to go into Youks for a wash-off at the old Roman baths. These baths were divided into small rooms, with water piped in from nearby springs, and you would walk down the steps into one of these rooms, turn the water on and fill the room to whatever height you desired. If you only wanted the water waist-deep, you could have that, and if you felt the urge to swim, that could be arranged also. As a rule, we stayed in the bath a long time, knowing it would be uncertain when we would be able to return for another overhauling of dirt. But actually we got so we didn't care. Sleeping in a foxhole immunizes one to odor. We never changed clothes and even if we had other clothes I doubt if we would have made the effort to change. We had two meals a day, breakfast and supper, and at each meal we got the inevitable powdered eggs, British tea, and hardtack. We surely missed the fresh eggs we had been able to buy from the natives down on the coastal regions. Here, in the mountains, not an egg was to be had.

When we weren't going on missions, we were taking care of the airplanes. We loaded the guns, filled the tanks with gasoline, using five gallon cans in the process, and it was a back-breaking job. The ground crews still had not arrived, and we were learning to

Major Glenn Hubbard, C.O. 94th Squadron, digging his own foxhole; Youks-Les-Bains, Algeria 1942.

have a new appreciation for the men who stayed behind and maintained the planes. The day that the ground crews joined us—arriving in all kinds of English, French, and American aircraft—it was a big reunion.

Faid Pass—December 2, 1942

One morning four of us were assigned to ground strafe the pill boxes and gun positions in the Faid Pass, which was a passage in the mountains on the road to Sfax. We were told to ground strafe this pass at precisely 7:30 A.M. and to stop strafing at exactly 7:35 A.M. at which time the ground troops would take over. The attack came off with clock-wise precision. At the end of five minutes when our ground strafing stopped, the ground troops had encircled the pass and immediately started rolling through. Our strafing had silenced the German guns almost at once, thus permitting the troops below to begin encircling, and while this was our first attempt, it proved there can be perfect coordination between ground troops and the air force.

We then proceeded to patrol on down the main road to Sfax and caught six trucks full of soldiers. It was just like an automatic

Crashed P-38 believed to be from 48th or 49th Squadron, 14th Fighter Group; Youks-Les-Bains, Algeria. December 1942.

On the wing of my P-38F-1 #41-7587; "Texas Terror / The Mad Dash." UN-O. Bill Lovell on the right of me. Note the cannon shell hole on the right cowling.

94th Squadron ground crew making boom repairs to my shot up P-38F-1 #41-7587, "Texas Terror / The Mad Dash." The ground crew did an amazing job of putting this airplane back together in such adverse conditions. Second from left is my Crew Chief, Roy Silvers. I am standing at the far right. (Credit - John Stanaway)

reflex the way we started ground strafing the trucks. In a matter of seconds all six of them were on fire. It was our first chance to shoot at trucks and I had the feeling I was shooting at targets, not men. Men were only coincidental.

One day shortly after our first encounter with the Germans, Roberts led a flight of four, including McWherter, Lovell, and myself. Our mission was to patrol the coast between Sfax and Gabes on the eastern coast of Tunisia. We were to shoot up any trucks, troops, or anything else we saw along the coastal road. We soon saw several trucks and tanks under a clump of trees about halfway down the road and in a few minutes left them all burning.

We continued flying low and as we approached the airdrome at Gabes—the same hot spot we had strafed several days before—Roberts yelled over the radio: "There's four of 'em taking off! I'll take the first one!" and he immediately turned and dived after the first ME-109 that was just taking off. Bill Lovell yelled that he would take the second one and I took out after the third while McWherter went for the fourth one. We were evenly matched except that we had the big advantages of altitude and speed on the four taking off.

And again it didn't seem hard to aim at the guy and push the button, which caused four .50 caliber machine guns and one 20-millimeter cannon to spurt several hundred bullets. The ME at which I was shooting had barely left the ground. He had just got his wheels up and gone into a bank, and he seemed to stay in the bank. Finally, his wing tip hit the ground and he cartwheeled into a flaming explosion.

Just about this same instant somebody yelled over the radio that six more had taken off while we had been engaged with the first four. I turned around sharply and dead ahead of me saw an ME spouting lead. I let loose with my guns and just about that time we whizzed by each other. The German had made a direct hit on the high pressure oil line of my right engine, and it didn't take but a few seconds for the engine to lose all its oil and freeze up. I feathered my prop to keep it from wind milling, and with my other engine made a determined effort to make myself scarce in this exciting atmosphere. It was some sixty miles back to base and I was going to make it or bust. I almost busted because two other ME's had seen what was happening and what I was trying to do, and started chasing me.

On one engine a P-38 was no match for a ME-109, either from the standpoint of a dogfight or for speed. With only one engine, going practically full power, I was only able to do about 275 m.p.h., as I was right down on the ground ducking in and out of the sand dunes. I started screaming for someone to come and help me and Bill Lovell radioed he was close behind and Roberts said he saw me and was trying to get over there.

94th Squadron flight line area, Youks-Les-Bains. Ground crews reading the ship for another mission. (Credit - Ken Sumney)

CHAPTER 4: North Africa

And there I had to sit, on my one engine, and let the two ME-109s make a couple of passes apiece at me. Just before the first German came in, Bill yelled to me over the radio: "Weave, Jack!"

And even though I did weave, the enemy made some hits on my plane. The radio went out and I was isolated. Lovell got on the tail of one of the Jerries and blasted him. The other ME ran away, probably not wishing to engage two P-38s.

Lovell and Roberts escorted me back to base. McWherter eventually came in by himself.

When I was able to lift myself out of the cockpit I realized that I was scared, shaking and weak. During the time the Germans were actually shooting at me, I kept wishing the damned thing would quit so I could set it down on the desert and get out of it, but the old reliable P-38 wouldn't quit. She kept running and took me right back to base where it was discovered I had many bullet holes in my plane—248 holes—including several large ones from the ground fire over the airdrome. A cannon shell had gone through my radio and lodged in the armor plate behind the seat, and it had torn the radio into several pieces. Another cannon shell had hit my propeller on the left engine—the good engine—causing a bad vibration in the running of that engine, and then another shell had hit the hydraulic fluid reservoir under my seat and left me ankle deep in fluid. And when I learned all of this I was good and scared.

I only made it back thanks to the timely intervention of my flight commander and his wingman. The left fuselage boom had been pretty badly damaged and the repair crew had to replace it with another scavenged from a junked P-38. When they came to connect the control cables that passed through the boom of the tail, they wouldn't quite stretch enough to make the connections, no matter how they tried. So they backed off and cut and spliced the cables to get the required length. The C.O. came by to inspect the plane and said to get Ilfrey to test fly it. The crew told him that they couldn't guarantee their splice job as it had been made under difficult conditions and without the proper equipment. His respone was to tell them not to worry..."that damn fool is going to kill himself anyway."

Officer's Mess - Biskra; December 1942. Extreme left - Lewis Murdock, extreme right - Dick McWherter.

94th Fighter Squadron's Enlisted Men's Mess; Biskra, North Africa; December 1942.

I was not told anything about the repair; not even to take it easy; I was just told to go ahead and make a test flight to see that everything works okay. I took off and started to wring out the P-38 over the field—loops, rolls, buzzing and all the rest. Everything checked fine. The repair crew was down on the ground watching my aerial display with great apprehension and were very relieved when I put the fighter down safely.

I was never informed about the splice job and continued to fly the plane without any problems. I'm sure the ground crew made an inspection after my test flight and probably kept a regular eye on it—but a case of the less said the better when it came to telling the pilot.

As for the C.O.'s comment, I know that I was one of his headaches, but I think that the repair crews could be relied upon to do a good job. It was not until 40 years later that I was informed about the incident at a Group Reunion!

We are Entertained by Sally of the Axis

Our lighter moments came at night when we heard Sally and Pete of the Axis broadcast from Tunis to the A.E.F. While Sally and Pete were supposed to make us homesick, we thoroughly enjoyed the American swing, and the pair was worth a lot to our morale. They relaxed and lulled us to sleep. Sally would tell us, over our powerful communications radio, how sorry she was for the poor boys out there on the hot, dry, dusty desert. (The desert was actually cold at night.) And she said she felt so sorry for us that she was going to play Glenn Miller's "The Little Brown Jug" just for us. After that Sally would ask us if we boys wouldn't love to be back in the U.S., riding on the Chattanooga Choo-Choo, and then the strains of "Chattanooga Choo-Choo" would come over the air, and, in all fairness to Sally, I have to admit she did succeed in making us a little homesick. Sally had a come-hither voice and I often wished she could have heard some of the remarks we made about her. She would have been more than flattered.

About all Pete did was to make cracks about President Roosevelt and his Jewish friends on Wall Street and make other absurd jokes.

Schedule for a day's combat mission. Umphrey, Pringle, Lovell, McWherter, Jones and Wilson were all killed in action. Sutcliffe was badly wounded in action. Widen became a Prisoner of War.

94th Squadron Operations Office, Biskra - December 1942. Bob Neale on left; Lewis Murdock taking off flight suit; I am sitting on the trunk.

In saying good-night, Sally would use her silkiest manner and beg us to lay down our arms, telling us we were already beaten, that we were going to lose, anyway, and to come on over to her side and be well-fed and taken care of in every way. When this was being written (summer of 1946), I read that Sally of the Axis, one American-born Rita Zucca, had been released from prison after serving not even a year of her light four-year term. She should have been strung up with the rest of 'em...

A Great General Visits Us
We were surprised one day when we saw the four stars on Gen. "Hap" Arnold's shoulders step out of an airplane, as we did not know at the time he was in North Africa for the Casablanca-Roosevelt conference. We were really elated to see him but his "pep" talk left us a little chilled. He said, "You're doing great, boys. If you continue to get them one for one, we'll win the war." We didn't go much for this "one for one" stuff.

Life on an Oasis
After several weeks at Youks-les-Bains sometime around the middle of December—we moved to the airdrome at Biskra to start performing missions again of high-level escorts of the big boys, the B-17s, which were just getting set up for operations.

The airdrome was on the edge of the oasis and was a flat field of hard sand, and here the ground crews and we pilots set up our tents among the date palms. We were glad to be out of the mud we had fought in the mountainous area surrounding Youks, and it was a relief to be free from the almost continuous rain. Before the war Biskra had been a winter resort of rich Europeans and was located behind the mountains on the edge of the Sahara Desert. It was hot and dusty during the day but the nights were cold and sometimes the temperature varied from sixty degrees to seventy degrees between day and night.

It looked like we were here to stay for a while and a lot of the men dug some pretty fancy fox holes for their homes. Several days

CHAPTER 4: North Africa

Following a night bombing attack by German Ju-88s this is all that remained of UN-T, a 94th Squadron P-38F-1.

Bombed out C-47 after a night bombing raid.

after our arrival, the Transatlantique Hotel in Biskra was taken over for the use of the pilots, and all we did was to just set up our bedrolls, with five of us in one room.

Each day we escorted the heavy bombers out to bomb targets from high altitudes like Tunis, Bizerte, Cagliari, Sardinia. Even though we were going on the offense in the enemy's territory and bombing, both the bombers and the fighters had to fight very much on the defense in order to return to base, because on almost every mission we were bounced by the Germans who were sitting up very high waiting for us, and we were lucky they were not able to put many fighters in the air, as we didn't have too many ourselves.

On these missions some of the boys were picking up a few hard-earned victories, and we were losing a few more men. I remember one occasion when our squadron of sixteen was bounced by a comparable number of Jerries and in the hairy dogfight we got split up. Williams, from Marietta, Ohio, was lost, and a long time afterwards we heard he was in a German prison camp.

Another day Rimke was leading our squadron on a mission. While we were escorting bombers near the target I noticed a lone B-17 far below us had dropped out of formation and was trying to head for home. It appeared that three or four Focke-Wulf 190s were making passes at him, doing their best to knock him down. I told Rimke this over the radio, and he told me to take my flight of four down to try and help the distressed B-17. Having the advantage of 8,000 to 10,000 feet on the Germans, we were able to dive down on them and I told my flight to pick out one each, and in turn I went after the one I had picked out. I must have caught the Jerry unaware as I made a good direct hit on him. He burst into flame. I saw Saul, my wing man, get one, and about that time I also saw two other Jerries in on him. I tried to get over to help him but the last I saw of Saul he was shooting at one Focke-Wulf and two were behind him, shooting at him, and the four disappeared into a cloud bank. Saul did not return that day and so far as I know nothing has ever been heard from him. Just as this was taking place, Bob Neale, who was near me, yelled there were two coming in on me. I evaded the attack as quickly as possible and in the ensuing dogfight Bob Neale's and my P-38 outperformed the two Focke-Wulfs and we were able to down both of the Jerries and confirm each other's victories. Then Neale and I teamed up to get the hell out of there because there were many more Focke-Wulfs than we had anticipated. We saw two P-38s below and dived to join them. They turned out to be McWherter and Murdock, and from the looks of the gathering of the Focke-Wulfs above, it appeared we were in for another dogfight, even though we were well separated from everyone else and we were low on ammunition and gasoline.

The four of us had been flying together for almost a year now and were very well versed on what each one was going to do. We knew we could depend on each other. Sure enough eight or ten Focke-Wulfs, who had altitude on us, came in for the attack. While we were able to weave in front of each other, warding off the attacks of these FWs, after several attacks we were able to outdistance them, as it would have been futile to have remained because the Jerries had everything on us: altitude, speed, and numbers.

When we got back to base that day we had lost three pilots. But we had more than trebled the losses in our victories. It is easy

Me and my P-38F-1 #41-7587; UN-O "Texas Terror / The Mad Dash."

94th Fighter Squadron P-38s in formation. It doesn't get any prettier than that...

to see how much more than friendship is required when your life depends on the actions of another pilot. It is a bond, it is something indefinable you can't write about and can't talk about. Friendships formed in combat are never forgotten.

This day proved to be a big day for the Allies as far as we in the Air Corps were concerned. The bombers and the fighters had over 20 confirmed victories, and for several weeks thereafter we were not bothered with the enemy, just annoyed. Now the enemy started coming to our base in groups of five or six at night, and one particular night about thirty plus JU-88s came over and really beat-up our field. In true American style, we all rushed to the top of the hotel to see what was taking place out at the field. The enemy scored direct hits that night on several B-17s and P-38s, and one 500 pounder hit right in the middle of our men's tent area, knocking down most of the tents, and scattering the squadron kitchen. Shrapnel from the bomb literally threw beans all over the place. It was sort of comical the next morning to see the boys, before putting up their tents again, really digging down deep into the earth and making foxholes to end all foxholes.

When a fighter pilot failed to return to base, there was no evidence of death. His plane simply didn't come back. A bomber was different. It brought men back to the base who would not know war any more. Writing about us and this particular day, Ernie Pyle, who had a room upstairs in the Hotel Transatlantique, said "Although our fighters in North Africa have accounted for many more German planes than we have lost, still our fighter losses are high. I have been chumming with a roomful of five fighter pilots for the past week... [Tonight] ...two of those five [are] gone."

Ernie Pyle was a quiet little fellow who wandered into our room one night, just to hear us talk of our day's activities. I don't believe

French Foreign Legion soldiers marching through the streets of Biskra. Taken from our balcony at the Hotel Transatlantique.

CHAPTER 4: North Africa

some of the boys knew who he was, but I had long read his column in the Houston Press and my mother had sent me clippings of the articles he had written while in England. He wrote several articles of life in Biskra, paid great tribute to the bombers and to the ground crews and troops, and I was surprised to find (several months after he had visited us) he had written a fine tribute to the fighter pilots, which included mention of me.

The following is an excerpt from Ernie Pyle's book, *This is Your War*; World Publishing Co.; 1943.

From Somewhere in French North Africa: In the Air
The boys were full of laughter when they told about it as they sat there on their cots in the dimly lighted room. I couldn't help having a funny feeling about them. They were all so young, so genuine, so enthusiastic. And they were so casual about everything—not casual in a hard, knowing way, but they talked about their flights and killing and being killed exactly as they would discuss girls or their school lessons.

Lieutenant Jack Ilfrey was a fine person and more or less typical of all the boys who flew our deadly fighters. He was from Houston, Texas and his father was a cashier of the First National Bank there. The family home was a 3122 Robinhood Street. Jack was only twenty-two. He had two younger sisters. He had gone to Texas A&M for two years, and then to the University of Houston, working at the same time for the Hughes Tool Company. He would soon be in the army for two years.

It was hard to conceive of his ever having killed anybody, for he looked even younger than his twenty-two years. His face was good-humored, his darkish hair was childishly uncontrollable and popped up into a little curlicue at the front of his head. He talked fast, but his voice was soft and he had a very slight hesitation in his speech that somehow seemed to make him a gentle and harmless person. There was not the least trace of the smart aleck or wise guy about him. He was wholly thoughtful and sincere. Yet he mowed 'em down.

In Africa, Ilfrey had been through the mill. He got two Focke-Wulf 190s one day, two Messerschmitt 109s another day. His fifth victory was over a twin-motored Messerschmitt 110, which carried three men. And he had another kill that had not been confirmed. He hadn't had all smooth sailing by any means. In fact, he was very lucky to be alive at all. He got caught in a trap one day and came home with many bullet holes in his plane. His armor plate stopped at least a dozen that would have killed him.

Jack's closet shave, however, wasn't from being shot at. It happened one day when he saw a German fighter duck into a cloud. Jack figured the German would pop out, and pop out he did - right into him, almost. They both kicked rudder violently, and they missed by practically inches. Neither man fired a shot, they were to busy about getting out of each other way. Jack said he was weak for an hour afterward.

There was nothing "heroic" about Lieutenant Ilfrey. He was afraid to run when that was the only thing to do. He told me about getting caught all alone one day at a low altitude. Two Germans got on his tail.

"I just had two choices," he said. "Either stay and fight, and almost surely get shot down, or pour everything I had to try and get away. Luckily the engine stood up." Ilfrey, like all the other men, had little in the way of entertainment and personal pleasure. I walked into his room late one afternoon, after he had come back from a mission, and found him sitting there at a table, all alone, killing flies with a folded newspaper. Our pilots really led lonely lives. There was nothing on earth for them to do but talk to each other. In two weeks a guy was talked out and after that it was just the same old conversation day after day.

The boys hung around the field part of the day, when they were not flying; then they would go to their rooms and lie on their bunks. They had read themselves and talked themselves out. There were no movies, no dances, no parties, no women—nothing. They just lay on their bunks.

"We've got so damn lazy we hardly bother to go to the toilet," one of them said. "We're no damn good for anything on earth any more except flying."

And yet people say being an ace was romantic. - from Ernie Pyle's "This is Your War."

Our room at the Hotel Transatlantique, Biskra - December 1942. Trying to drink some of that awful French stuff...

Bill Lovell (right) and I eating lunch on the desert. (Credit - Ken Sumney)

With my ground crew; Roy Silvers, Crew Chief (second from right); McGinnes, Armorer (far right). Biskra, January 1943.

In contrast to Ernie Pyle was Frederick C. Painton, correspondent for Readers' Digest. Painton was a big, robust fellow who loved his drinks. He would come into our room, and we'd play the ukulele, and Painton, being very boisterous, would sing loudest. He was such a big, heavy man it was hard to realize he had made a parachute jump with the paratroops when Africa was invaded. Despite his bulk, he did all that was required of a correspondent on the front. We liked Painton a hell of a lot. He was a regular guy.

Death hit home when Dick McWherter was killed. He was one of my best friends in the squadron. We had been together for almost two years—through flying school, in England, and to the end in North Africa. War leaves scars which are hard to erase.

A few days after Dick's death, Bugs Lentz, who was on a patrol near Tripoli, was shot down by ground fire. Out of the original six of us, who had been in flying school together and who had joined the 94th Fighter Squadron together, there were now only Bob Neale and myself left. We began to feel the process of elimination was progressing pretty rapidly.

About six weeks after Lentz's disappearance, he suddenly arrived at base in a British bomber from Malta. He had quite a story to tell.

It seems when he was hit he was able to crash land his airplane and suffered no physical damage in doing so. He was soon captured by the Italians and taken into Tripoli, questioned by the Germans and put in prison. After several weeks of confinement he was put aboard an Italian submarine, along with eleven other Allied prisoners, five Britishers, and six Americans. All eleven of them were crammed into a small room in the submarine and were being taken to Italy. When we were a day or so out of Tripoli—halfway to Italy—the submarine had to ride on the surface due to rough water, and in a short time after surfacing, a small British flotilla sighted the Italian sub and started shelling it. Lentz said they didn't know exactly what was going on, but they had a good idea and after several minutes of shelling the sub seemed to be pretty badly damaged. The Italians went wild and there was nothing but confusion on the submarine. The eleven Allied prisoners had to overpower their guards to get up on deck and when they reached the deck, they found the Italians abandoning ship. They were unable to get any life belts and everybody except Lentz and one of the Britishers jumped overboard. The two let themselves down on ropes to the water's level on the side of the sub which was not being shelled. They clung there for thirty or forty minutes while the British continued shelling, and just before dark it sank, the two men pushed off from the sub and swam around, treading water, until the British

A testament to the rugged Lockheed P-38. This 94th FS Lightning #422092, UN-C, was flown by Lt. Benton Miller. The aircraft hit a telephone pole while strafing a German convoy. It managed to return to the base at Biskra. The impact knocked off the left propeller and oil cooler; bent the main spar into an early day dihedral configuration. Note the 97th BG B-17 in the background.

CHAPTER 4: North Africa

The Garden of Allah, a small plot of oasis at Biskra.

My folks back in Houston, Christmas Day 1942. Mother and Father, sisters Ruth and Betty, taking care of my car.

picked them up ten minutes later. The boat that the British sent out for rescue picked up Lentz and his companion first and when the crew saw one was an Englishman and the other an American, they were in quite a sweat for a few minutes, until Lentz explained they had been prisoners on the Italian sub. The Britisher and Lentz were the only two out of the eleven prisoners who were saved. Nearly all the Italians survived.

I had heard of the Garden of Allah and from the advance publicity, I expected it to be a big bunch of glamour, and I had the same let-down feeling about it that I had when I first saw Hollywood. The Garden of Allah, in my language, was just a little park with a little wall around it. Actually, the garden was just a heavily vegetated spot, with a stream of water running through, and surrounded by a wall. It might possibly compare with parts of Griffith Park in Los Angeles, and this could be stretching the imagination a shade far. I did not see any beauty and thought its one ironic distinction was that this highly vegetated piece of ground was enclosed by the desert.

The beautiful greenery of the Garden of Allah.

One day while Lovell and I were sitting on the balcony of our room at the Transatlantique, which overlooked the main street running into Biskra, we saw two French officers on horseback coming down the street and behind them was a small group of Arabs. It was quite evident that a serious argument was going on between the officers and the Arabs. One Arab kept pulling at the coat of one of the officers, and he would try to knock him away. When they were right out in front of our balcony, the Arab jumped up and spat in the officer's face.

To our utter amazement, the officer whipped out his saber and with one quick, hard swing completely severed the Arab's head from his body.

We sat there, stupefied, and watched the headless body squirt a fountain of blood from the neck, take a step or two, and fall. The two French officers calmly continued down the street. In a few minutes the other Arabs, who had somewhat scattered during the beheading, returned and picked up the body and head.

We were still unable to talk as we had never in all our lives seen anything like this, and Umphrey finally made the remark how even though something of a similar nature might happen back in the States, the instigator could never have got away with it. It was easy to see, from this decapitation, how a handful of French militarists had been able to control these millions of illiterate Arabs. Democratic principles did not apply here, and now with the arrival and occupation by the Americans and our free and equal ideas, the whole French system of control was getting out of order. It was something to think about.

When we were in the mood we would go down into the native quarter of Biskra and watch the French hootchie-kootchie girls dance. The stench was pretty bad in the places in which these shows were held, and the women had protruding stomachs—along the malnutrition line—and they'd never inspire G.I.s to moral turpitude. The Arab men would group around the dancers, watch a little while, and then walk out. Music was made on a lute, a gourd, a bamboo fife, a sheepskin tom-tom, and a tambourine, and this weird

LEFT: General Atkinson presenting D.F.C. to the members of 94th Squadron. Standing to the left of me - Clifford Molzahn, Wesley Pringle, Donald Starbuck, Lewis Murdock. On my right - Bob Neale, Jim Harman, Newell Roberts, Col. Ralph Garman, 1st Fighter Group C.O., is behind General Atkinson. Biskra - February 1943.

mixture was accompanied by the natives' monotonous chanting. It sounded like snake charmer's music at a circus to me and the whole thing was as dull as the day after Christmas, but it was something to do for an hour or two.

Christmas Day '42 was just another routine day, which we spent escorting bombers. After we returned from our mission a few of the pilots scouted around and brought in a fifty-gallon keg of Muscatel wine and the enlisted men and pilots proceeded to have a knocked-out Christmas. If one has ever been drunk on wine, he would probably never repeat the performance. I had had the experience and knew when to stop that night but some of the boys didn't, and they had hangovers that lingered over into the second and third day. But that night is one I'll remember. I've never heard so many Christmas dinners splattering in the halls of a hotel...

However, the following day was quite a different story. While leading a flight in the Bizerte-Tunis area, I saw some FW-190s attacking a crippled American bomber. With the advantage of altitude, I dove down and picked one out. He turned and went out over Lake Bizerte, but I stayed on his tail. I got some good hits and soon put him into smoke and flame. Just as he was about to hit the water,

Monday, December 28, 1942

Jack Ilfrey Bags His Fifth Plane in Fight Over Africa

By Associated Press
Algiers, Dec. 28.—Lt. Jack Ilfrey of Houston, United States fighter pilot, shot down two German Focke-Wulf 190s which attacked a Flying Fortress during a raid Sunday on Bizerte and became one of the highest scoring American pilots, with five victories to his credit.

When he had finished off the second enemy three other Axis planes dived toward him but he eluded them.

* * *

Lieutenant Ilfrey's two-plane bag of Sunday qualifies him as an ace, since he now has five planes to his credit. The public relations office of Ellington Field stated Monday that the qualifications used during World War I were five enemy planes credited to the pilot, and that the number had not been changed.

Lieutenant Ilfrey is the son of Mr. and Mrs. F. W. Ilfrey, 3122 Robinhood. He is a native of Houston and graduated from Lamar High School in 1938, entering Texas A. and M. the following autumn, where he took flight instruction. He also attended the University of Houston. He had a private pilot's license and an instructor's rating when he enlisted in the air corps in May, 1941, as a flying cadet. He received his primary training at Ryan Field, California, and graduated from Luke Field, Arizona.

In July he was sent to England and he participated in the raid on Lille, France, in October. From letters which have passed the censor, his mother believes there are possibly other victories to his credit in addition to the five listed in the story from Algiers.

This article appeared in the *Houston Chronicle*, December 28, 1942. I didn't know about it until a month after it had been published.

NOW AN ACE

First Lt. Jack Ilfrey bagged two German Focke-Wulf 190's to qualify as an ace, since he now has five enemy planes to his credit. The picture was taken shortly after he received his wings and commission as second lieutenant. He was promoted to first lieutenant while in England.

CHAPTER 4: North Africa

48th Squadron, 14th Fighter Group. December 1942. They were also stationed with us at Youks-Les-Bains.

I saw machine-gun bullets kicking up in the water in front of me and knew that a bandit was on my tail. I banked and turned as hard as I could. As my speed became slower than his, my circumference of turn was smaller, and with a great burst of throttles to the engines I came up under him with my guns blazing. He nose dived into the lake, giving me a double victory and my fifth kill—thus making me the first ace of the 94th.

It was common practice for pilots who scored a victory to do a roll over the field upon return—provided the plane wasn't damaged—to let the ground men know of the success. Of course, it was in my nature to have to try and do something more spectacular, so I made a habit of diving down, buzzing across the field, pull up, do my roll and then pull up into a half loop, rolling out at the top. The Group C.O., Lt. Col. Ralph Garman, didn't like this exhibition too much, even though he knew it was good for the ground crew's morale.

The day I got the double victory, and, feeling my P-38 was in good shape, I was going balls-out on the deck, pulled up and did a double roll and on into a half loop when an engine quit. I had the plane on its back and was just starting to roll out; no airspeed to speak of, ground not far below me; and I liked to have lost it. Well, I survived a really close shave. Even though I had just become his first ace, Garman was livid. Restricted me to quarters and cut off my liquor allowance. After a good reprimand and my promise not to do it again I was back hunting Jerries. But, of course, I had to think up some other trick. Returning from a mission soon afterwards, I buzzed the Colonel's headquarters tent which was near some palm trees at the edge of the field. I must have been a little too low for, as I pulled up, I saw Garman run out, and shake his fist and jump into his Jeep. As I landed and taxied in to park, the Colonel's Jeep got behind me and collected a lot of the dust my props were throwing up. By the time I'd got out and was about to jump off the wing to meet the stern-faced Garman, I was pretty sure I was going to be grounded or transferred. At that moment a command car drove up and out popped General Pete Quesada from 12th Air Force HQ. He was laughing up a storm! Instead of being chewed out, I was presented with a fifth of scotch by the General (in appreciation of my knocking down five Jerries) while I listened to him reminding my Colonel how he, Garman, had pulled various stunts when as a Lieutenant he flew under Quesada's command back in the "thirties." Despite my "free spirit," Ralph Garman later gave me the best letter of recommendation I ever received in the service.

This was just one more example of what one of the regular pranksters termed "foolin' around syndrome"; more truly defined as an uninhibited zest for non-conformity.

Hollywood Comes to the Desert

One fine day in January a C-47 cargo plane dropped into Biskra and out jumped the most beautiful cargo we had seen since leaving England: Kay Francis, Carol Landis, Mitzi Mayfield and Martha Raye. The girls put on several wonderful performances and every-

94th Squadron Operations Office. Four replacements pilots are shown here. Bugs Lentz (standing) and Newell Roberts (sitting).

USO show at Biskra, North Africa - January 1943. Martha Raye is shown on stage with Eddie Bigham on piano.

Rest camp for fatigued combat pilots - Agadir, French Morocco, 250 miles below Casablanca.

On the beach below our hotel - (left to right) Lewis Murdock, Unknown, me, Newell Roberts. Others in the photo are believed to be 82nd Fighter Group pilots.

body was impressed with Martha Raye singing "Queenie—the Cutie of the Burlesque Show"; and before the quartet left we were all singing "Queenie." (P.S. For weeks after Carol Landis left, our memories drooled.)

Shortly afterwards some badly needed replacements of pilots and planes came in. We had been scraping the bottom of the barrel to get enough planes in the air, and we had reached the bottom of the barrel when it came to pilots. Ten of us were given a sorely needed rest and were flown in a transport several hundred miles over to the resort town of Agirdir, below Casablanca, on the Atlantic Coast. On the way we stopped in Algiers for a day and who should we run into but Major Sherry, our old group intelligence officer, who had been transferred to General Spaatz's headquarters. He invited a couple of us to go out with him to the general's villa for lunch. We felt a little out of place because our dress uniforms were dirty and full of wrinkles, having been packed away for months, and our shoes were unshined, but General Spaatz put us at ease and all the brass seemed very much interested in our work.

We met Elliott Roosevelt, who was a lieutenant colonel at that time. He had done some good work in establishing the route over which we had flown the North Atlantic and his photo "Joes" did excellent work later back in England. Elliott was surprisingly quiet.

The good food was a real treat, and the dishes, napkins, and silverware made us feel civilized again.

Rest and Recuperation

Agirdir compared favorably with the climate of Florida in the wintertime, but certainly not with all the luxuries. We were housed in a very nice hotel, had more varied food than we had been accustomed to getting. We lay around on the beach, went horseback riding, played volleyball, and one day we went down a hundred miles or so to a place called Tiznit, which was a French Foreign Legion garrison. It looked exactly like the garrisons you see in the movies, surrounded by high walls, lonely and isolated. The French officers entertained us royally and gave us an elaborate feed, with plenty of cognac, anisette, and Calvados. The Arab women put on a special

Lewis Murdock and Donald Starbuck. Lewis had been a Virginia Horseman and took groups of willing pilots on fox hunts. He also spoke French, which came in very handy in French North Africa.

TIZNIT - Entrance to the French Foreign Legion garrison.

CHAPTER 4: North Africa

Interior of the TIZNIT garrison.

Exit of the garrison.

chanting dance for us, with practically just a sash around the stomach and flutes supplying the music.

The ten days at Agirdir were all too short and then back to the old grind again. Things were easier at Biskra. The replacements reduced our having to fly so much, and we were the leaders now instead of just the flyers.

Margaret Bourke-White came to visit us on the base and took a lot of pictures of the boys in the fighter squadron. Margaret had come to North Africa the hard way. She had landed with the invasion forces at Oran and was minus all her clothes and equipment, as the boat which was carrying her to Africa was sunk, and here in Biskra she was traipsing around in a flying suit. She was interested in everything, what we were doing and thinking, and even went so far as to fly in a B-17 to see what a raid was all about. She was a photographer for Life magazine, and I was mentioned in the August 16, 1943 issue.

Wes Gallagher also came to Biskra and I had occasion to talk with him about some of my experiences, and again I was surprised to find myself mentioned in his book, "Back Door to Berlin." This surprise, of course, came months later.

Constantine

The Siroccan winds started blowing in off the Sahara Desert, bringing in tons of sand, and preparations were made for us to leave Biskra. It was impossible for us to operate with the sand doing its best to defeat every single movement. We were separated from the bombers and moved on to a small fighter strip of our own near Constantine, which became our Twelfth Air Force headquarters.

At Our Base, Chateau Dun Du-Rhumel, we got back into tents with four to six officers living in one pyramidal tent. It was early February and still pretty cold in the mountains. We had our own homemade stove which we had concocted by taking a five gallon gasoline can, cutting the bottom out and placing it over a little pile of rocks. For a chimney we took smaller (empty) cans of beans, peas, etc. and cutting out the tops and bottoms, we had our chimney. Outside the tent we placed a can of gasoline at a higher level than the stove and the gasoline was fed by pipes (small copper tubing) that led to the stove. The gasoline dripped on the rocks, burned, and we had fire. We produced lights in the tents by means of a portable generator and by connecting a speaker into our tent, which was attached to our big communications radio, we were still able to hear Sally and Pete and their Nazi nonsense.

We now had heat, lights, and music, and with our stove we could have hot water helmet baths instead of cold water wash-offs, which we avoided. Eggs were plentiful in Constantine and whenever we received a ration of British cheese, we made soufflés; now and then we had French toast. Once in a while an Arab goat would accidentally get in front of a jeep and that night we'd have barbecued goat. It was only coincidental that it always turned out to be a young and tender goat.

Our missions changed a little bit and we went back to ground strafing. Rommel and his armies were on the Mareth Line, and we spent whole days strafing them on the open roads. At this time Montgomery's Eighth Army coming from Tripoli, was pushing

Talking with Margaret Bourke - White, well known *Life Magazine* photo - journalist.

The suspension bridge at Constantine - *quite often it was found in our landing pattern.*

Six of the original 94th Squadron pilots. Of the six men, four were killed in action, one was listed as missing in action, one survived the war (*now deceased*).

Rommel's armies back up our way and forcing our ground troops to retreat. As a last desperate effort, Rommel tried to surge through Kasserine Pass and take Tebessa, which was the arsenal of this section of the front. Had Rommel taken Tebessa, it would have been disastrous for us, as we would have lost all we had gained on landing at this front.

On the day of the Battle of Kasserine Pass, twelve of us were assigned to ground strafe through the pass. Even one year later when I was flying over Germany with the Eighth Air Force, I don't believe I ever saw so much flak. It seemed to come from everywhere, not only from below but from the hills above the pass, down on us. Of the twelve pilots, only eight of us got through the pass. Four were lost in the pass, two of the boys managed to make our lines and crash land, and six of us were able to get our P-38s back to base, but we all had battle damage. We had lost Rimke, one of our old veterans.

Again our reaction to this raid was that if the Germans wanted this godforsaken place that bad—let 'em have it! We learned later that the concentrated air attack on Kasserine Pass that day helped to turn the tide of battle.

It looked like the air force had at last decided on what would constitute a combat tour of duty. Up to this time we had had nothing to look forward to. It just seemed to be a process of elimination. Out of our original squadron of 27 flyers who had left the States some ten months previously, only eight of us were left, and to finish off our time, we started flying easy, light missions. About the only thing we could think of was when we had 200 combat hours or 50 missions we would be eligible to be taken off combat flying.

Thomas White from Kelso, Washington, a P-38 pilot from the 82nd Fighter Group, and myself were called to Algiers, as the leading American aces with confirmed victories, to appear on Winston Burdette's CBS Sunday broadcast (see Appendix 1). Although we were the top scoring pilots at the time, we were soon surpassed by other pilots, some of them having as many as twelve or thirteen victories when North Africa capitulated. Victories down here were harder earned than later on up in England and France. We only received credit for planes destroyed in the air, while a year or so later planes destroyed on the ground were also counted as victories.

At the time the fighters were flying weather missions. On these missions we observed the altitude and the density of clouds, formation of vapor trails, and where the freezing level was located. The data we obtained determined where the bombers would go that day.

The weather trip I took before breakfast one morning was an eye-opener. I got up before daylight and flew over to Sardinia and Sicily and came back over Tunisia to the base at Constantine. In three and a half hours I had flown over four countries, taken notes of the weather all along the way, and had returned to base in time for breakfast. The Mediterranean Sea looked blue and peaceful that morning and there was nothing to disturb the tranquility of my flight before breakfast.

The weather flights controlled the destiny of the people over whose countries we had flown and my reports that morning would determine the course the B-17s would take and the fate of these people. I don't know whether I felt important or not. If I did, it was wrong.

Street scene in Cairo - April 1943.

CHAPTER 4: North Africa

Cairo Taxicab with Doc Young.

One of our boys failed to return from a weather flight, and we never found out whether he was jumped by enemy fighters, had engine troubles, or had got lost and landed in the Mediterranean.

Constantine appeared to be the most foreign-like city we had seen so far. It was really two cities built on very high cliffs, connected by a large suspension bridge. Constantine was built in the olden days when cities were built on cliffs to prevent seizure by the enemy. At night we visited the casino where there was music, liqueurs, and girls to dance with, and girls. . .

The day for my last mission arrived and it was so routine you could almost term it casual. I knew nothing could happen to me on this patrol trip in the straits between Tunisia and Sicily. At this time the Germans were trying to get supplies into Rommel's armies, which were being closed into a gap. And we were to spot and report on any shipping activities we saw in the straits. Several miles off Cape Bon we were scouting along at around 600 feet below some low, overhanging clouds when I noticed some balloons flying right under the cloud level, and at the same instant I noticed these balloons were flying from a convoy of ships. And almost immediately I saw a JU-87 Stuka below and to the left of us. Quinn, my only companion, saw it about the same time that I did and I told him to go in and get a shot at it and that I would follow him. Then I saw another JU-87 or ME-110 'way off to the right, and just as Quinn was getting the JU-87 lined up in his sight, I turned and found myself practically staring into six to eight ME-109s. I didn't look twice. Although I thought I was a seasoned P-38 pilot, I knew we were no match for them. I yelled to Quinn, "Let's get the hell out of here", and he was in complete agreement. We tore off, "balls out," ducking around the clouds, and streaking for home with the Germans now on our tails. Fortunately, our airplanes were faster than those of the Jerries, but we still had several hundred miles to go across enemy territory, and we could not have lasted very long, going full throttle. The gasoline would have soon played out. We sweated along and I sweated out my forthcoming leave home. In fact, when we got into our own lines, I had sweated out the alphabet.

When we got back to base we made our report and in less time than it takes to tell about it, the bombers had taken off and were successful in destroying the convoy before it reached the coast. It was still a battle, however, as the convoy was well protected.

I could now think about my leave in earnest. I had completed mission number 72, had 228 hours of combat flying time, and six confirmed enemy planes. The eight of us started sweating out for the day to come when we could leave for home.

Unexpected Travel

While waiting around for our orders to come through, transferring us to the States—we hoped—Shelton, Young and I decided to hitchhike a ride on a transport to Tripoli, which was now in the hands of the Allies. We did not encounter any difficulty in getting to Tripoli and landed at the Casa Benita Airdrome just outside of the city, and we stayed there for a few days.

This was our first glimpse into the havoc which had been wrought by our B-17s. The airdrome was a shambles. We saw several hundred German planes which had been destroyed on the ground. Tripoli itself was a typical dirty Italian town. There were a few streetcars running and the harbor was full of sunken vessels. It was springtime and there were great profusions of wild flowers growing everywhere. The Italians were friendly and greasy and the little children haunted us with the same old cry: "Cigarette! Candy!"

It was here in Tripoli I met a friend of mine with whom I had gone through flying school. He was flying a transport and was on his way to Cairo, and he asked us why we didn't come along. So we decided, without too much official permission, to make the trip. On this flight we passed over the famous battlefields of Montgomery's Eighth Army, the Marble Arch, Halfaya Pass, Tobruk, Bengazi, and El Alamein.

As we flew into the Land of the Egyptians nothing but desert and wasteland greeted us. The transition came as we neared the Nile River Valley. Everything was a beautiful, fertile green, and it was a refreshing change from the yellow sand and sand dunes.

We landed at the airdrome, Heliopolis, and suddenly I came up with the realization that Cairo was just about halfway around the world from Houston. Houston . . . I hoped I'd be seeing it soon.

Postcard that I bought in Cairo. The Arabic writing says "The World's Greatest Democrats."

For no reason at all, I was surprised to see streetcars and automobiles. Cairo hit you with a rush. Everywhere you saw Arabs, Egyptians, European refugees, Germans, Italians, Americans, French, and New Zealanders. . . the most cosmopolitan city we'd yet been in. It was a curious city, too. You felt overtones of darkness, and whether they existed or not, shadows seemed to hover over you . . . a new world . . . a strange, completely alien world to an American. The dark Senegalese captured my imagination with their colorful sashes and robes.

For the first time in almost a year we found everything we wanted—at a price. It was wonderful to enjoy candy bars and ice cream. You could rent automobiles, there was plenty of gasoline, and you thought of home because things were plentiful here. I bought a Swiss watch for thirty dollars, which would have cost sixty-five or seventy dollars Stateside. We loaded up with heavy Egyptian silver bracelets, and all kinds of ornate jewelry. Trading was brisk with the Egyptians. . .they'd trade diamonds and silver for any gold we had. But we were skeptical of everything. The Egyptians had no talent for inspiring confidence or trust—against those dark overtones. . .

Had you been in the Hotel Continental the second night of our stay in Cairo, you would have seen at least the first cousin to a glutton. We feasted on steak, well-prepared vegetables (a real treat), and at the end of the meal, we had ice cream. It was good ice cream and we weren't content until we had had several helpings. The Egyptian waiters spoke English and were suave creatures.

That night we found a congenial Egyptian, speaking no less than seven languages, who took us to Madame Badia's, the most famous nightclub in Cairo. The most I can say for Madame's place is that it was flush, plush, and swank, and prices were based on the American scale. In short, this means top prices were topped. Madame herself was a faded-out version of Sophie Tucker, without Sophie's raucous charm. Now the girls at Madame's were something different. These little Egyptian cuties were pretty, well-formed, and when they danced you thought of the slinking babes who used to entertain Cleopatra on the days when she was tired. Their stripteases were done with a deadliness that did not leave you in doubt, and later on after the place closed, you appreciated that a first-class psychological job had been done. Upon waking in the morning came the cold, hard fact that the evening had cost at least a fourth interest in the Bank of England.

When we started out to see the Pyramids we got a dragoman (guide). You needed a dragoman if only for the purpose of keeping all the other dragomen from pursuing you. The streetcar ride across the Nile River was nice and when we came to the end of the line, it was but a short walk to the place where other guides had camels for rent—and there was no getting out of renting one of these smelly animals. I had pictured the Sphinx as something terrific. The first shock came when we mounted camels and rode on a modern paved road right up to the Pyramids.

Somehow the paved road was completely out of place. It struck the wrong note. And the Sphinx, well, the less said the better.

As far as I am concerned, the "Rock" is a racket and the expedition left me numb with boredom.

When we arrived at the Sphinx still another guide had to be hired to show us through the Temple. For a small fortune, you could have your pictures taken in front of the Sphinx, and when we whipped out our own cameras and started snapping pictures of each other, you should have seen the consternation written on the faces of those Egyptians. They had been gypped but only temporarily. We rode over to the Pyramids and found we had to buy up another guide to lead us into the burial rooms. After this, we dispensed with all guides and said good-bye to King Tut and his present extortioners.

I met Rosa that night in Gippy's. The atmosphere in Gippy's might have had something to do with my seeing Rosa. It was an open air nightclub, with a patio, and all the romantic trappings. The orchestra played American tunes and the club was crowded with Americans, Australians, and New Zealanders. The Australians pulled off some big fights before the evening was over. They seemed to be the rough ones.

Rosa was a cute little girl from Trieste with lots of vim, vigor and vitality. She claimed to be a refugee and I could well believe this, considering how she clung. She danced in the American way and while her English wasn't very good, it didn't matter. We got along. Her apartment was nice and I wasn't bothered with my two companions that night. From then on we had a permanent guide for the few remaining days we stayed in Cairo.

The bazaars in Cairo were located on narrow, dirty streets in the native section and the ugliness of the streets was in sharp contrast to the beautiful things offered for sale. We bought perfumes, embroidered cloths, more jewelry, and when we left we fairly staggered under our load of souvenirs. We saw the Citadel which in years past had been used to guard the old city of Cairo.

We almost didn't go into one of the mosques because we had to take off our shoes before entering, and we were a little ashamed to show our socks. No mother would have been proud of our socks—there were holes and then more holes.

Early one night we all went to a very modern and very international theatre in Cairo. The audience was predominately British but

Sphinx and the Pyramids, Cairo, Egypt - April 1943. (Left to right) Charles Shelton, Dragoman (guide), Doc Young and me.

CHAPTER 4: North Africa

One of the sickening sights of North Africa. Two beggar caste. (Credit - Ken Sumney)

the movie was an American one with English being spoken on the screen. Underneath, on another screen, the captioned dialogue flashed in French. Off to one side the Arabic letters raced across the little screen, and off to the other side was the Egyptian screen. During intermission we were allowed to smoke and it was really something to see the roof part in the middle and see the sky and the stars and watch the smoke go out.

When we started to go back to base we thought the Ninth Air Force was going to give us a little trouble just because we didn't have any leave papers on us. Luckily, we met another friend who was going back to Tripoli on a transport and we were equally lucky in getting another transport out of Tripoli for Algiers.

When we got back to Algiers there were no orders out yet for us to go home, and we were assigned to ferrying P-38s from the assembly area at Oran to the fighter squadrons up front. On one occasion I led six P-38s on a 4,000-mile trek to New Delhi, India. Our flight took us across Tunisia, Libya, Egypt, Arabia, and on into India. It was a rush trip and we did not get to see much of India. One thing stood out, however—the filth and the malnutrition of the natives. It was hard to imagine how people lived under such conditions. I'd give an American two weeks to survive.

At New Delhi I ran across another transport friend of mine who was getting ready to fly the Hump, and he asked me to come along as his copilot, unofficially of course. It was a long, hard trip and I could easily see how bored the pilots must have been in flying the Hump. We landed at Chunking just long enough to get some food and sleep and then back to New Delhi where a transport took us six pilots back to Algiers, with several stops; but the only place we had an opportunity to look over was Tel Aviv. It was a revelation to see the modern buildings, with plate glass windows and indirect lighting. The town was clean and everywhere you saw green growing things.

There were still no orders for us when we got back to base and while I was waiting for my papers to come through I decided I'd go to Casablanca and really see the town this time. I took a buddy along with me and we put up in grand style at the Hotel Sueiss. This hotel is located on the beach, just below Casablanca, and it was wonderful to be able to get up in the morning and go swimming. I had good food again and I don't think I'll ever take good food for granted again. All I have to do is to think of powdered eggs, dates, and hardtack to be appreciative of a piece of well-made toast.

Casablanca was a lot different from Algiers. It was flat and spread out in all directions. There were plenty of natives but the French predominated. We looked all over Casablanca for Rick's Place but never found it. (Humphrey Bogart, please explain.) Here we saw many European refugees—they seemed to be everywhere— and here also we saw lawlessness at its worst. There was no safety after night. You could have a knife stuck in your back without half trying, and the police gave you no protection at all. Security was unknown in Casablanca.

The day finally arrived and I could hardly believe I was on a transport plane, coming home. You have a feeling (when you're in the army) anything can happen (and it usually does) to upset your plans. But everything was going smoothly and it promised to be a wonderful trip.

The passengers aboard were interesting and varied. There were enlisted men from the Middle Eastern Area—the Eighth Army— and several army nurses who had been stationed in India and who were going home because they had been a little impetuous and had decided to raise a family without benefit of clergy. George Nixon, the well-known correspondent for I.N.S., was on the plane, headed for a new assignment.

Our first stop was at Marrakesh, the scene of President Roosevelt's Casablanca conference, and a beautiful resort town, with low buildings made of brown stone, which were covered by bougainvillea vines. I got a fleeting glimpse of Dakar when we stopped for refueling, and at Accra, on the Gold Coast of Africa, I saw my first African blacks. I had been living on the Dark Continent for about six months, and because I had not seen any Negroes, it was hard to feel I was in Africa. My imagination must have demanded blacks and tom-toms. The airdrome at Accra was right on

Hotel Suisse - Casablanca

59

the beach, and for a shilling these magnificent-looking black people would take you out on surfboards and give you a real thrill.

The next day we flew on to the Ascension Islands. This volcanic spot was barren of everything, including trees, and we felt sorry for the boys who were stationed there. One of my good friends, Billy Archer, was stationed there. Then on we went, down below the equator to Natal, Brazil, where we spent the night and where I bought a pair of South American boots and an alligator band for my watch.

The fourth day found us in Belem, at the mouth of the Amazon River. We spent the night there and it was my first experience sleeping in tropical surroundings. Both the airdrome and sleeping quarters were built among the trees, in the most gorgeous foliage imaginable. By next afternoon we were in Port-au-Spain, Trinidad, and after refueling, we flew on up to the western tip of Puerto Rico, where we spent the night. The army air base looked good to us and the officers' club looked still better with its delicious food and rum and Coca-Cola. It was the first Coca-Cola I had tasted since leaving the States, and it's not necessary to add that full justice was done to both rum and Coca-Cola. I bought a jug of Puerto Rican rum as a souvenir to bring home, which the customs officers in Miami took away from me because I had overlooked affixing the proper stamp or something.

It was beautiful weather all the way from Puerto Rico up through the Bahama Islands to Miami. We could see the coast of Florida a long way off, and even though most of our homes were far from the Peninsula State, it was still home to us.

Entering Casablanca. We all looked for Rick's Place, but we were unable to locate the famous watering hole. At the time, Casablanca was the crossroads between East and West, a Nazi world and a free world. There were lost souls from every corner of the world. Eisenhower's early headquarters for the North African Campaign.
It symbolized intrigue, romance and hopes for freedom because of its location.

5

STATESIDE AT LAST

We were wild to get out of the plane at Miami, but the customs officers compelled us to sit for a couple of hours while they sprayed the airplane, disinfected every nook and corner, and gave us inoculations. We were practically maniacs by the time we threw ourselves into a taxi and raced to town.

Gasoline rationing had not gone into effect at the time we left the States, and from all reports and from what we had read in the English newspapers and also in the Stars and Stripes, we thought there would be practically no automobiles on the street. We had been given a big build-up about only four gallons a week being allowed motorists. Our first big shock in Miami was to see hordes of automobiles crowding the streets and when we saw just the driver alone in the car, we wondered about the propaganda we had heard, such as "Ride alone and you ride with Hitler." We noticed there were more "B" and "C" stickers than "A," and decided that gasoline rationing was a phony.

We made the driver stop at Walgreen's on the way to the barracks at the army air base and got a banana split. It was wonderful. There was a bar across the street and we dashed over for a quickie. It, too, was wonderful. Our appetites had just begun to function, so we asked the taxi driver where we could find a good steak. After we had had our fill, we dashed out to the PX at Miami Beach and were overcome at the size of this PX and what it had to offer. I was practically threadbare, so I bought khaki clothes for the summer and loaded up with all the things I had been needing for months.

That night in Miami was something out of this world. We peeled off into every bar which got in our way. First, we celebrated for being back on U.S. soil, then we celebrated for the sake of celebration, and after that we just celebrated.

It was a weary captain who climbed aboard the airliner next morning, headed for Houston. I had not told my family I was back in the States, so when I got to New Orleans I called my mother over long distance and told her I would be in Houston within an hour and a half. She almost fainted on me but somehow she managed to notify all the relatives in town, and when I arrived at the Municipal Airport, I was flat knocked out by the delegation of relatives and friends awaiting me. It was old home week wrapped up in a month's package. I had as many questions to ask as my family had to ask me. I wanted to know if my car was still running, if my mother was going to have liver and onions for dinner, and when I was reassured on these two points I felt better.

Here I was back in my hometown. My folks had never really expected me to come back. Houston was unchanged, in the main. We had two large shipbuilding companies now, Ellington Field was full of soldiers, and Houstonians were going about their usual ways, seemingly little concerned about the war. In fact, in talking with people, you'd hardly know men were being killed all over the world. And some people seemed to think I had had a grand old time, had lived a glamorous life. It was useless to try to explain about North Africa. Civilian comprehensions didn't go that far.

Invitations poured in. I was interviewed by the local papers and journalistically was the hero of the moment, all of which left me feeling it was being overdone, that the full significance was not even faintly realized. I made a speech at a ship-launching and met the Sullivans whose five sons went down on the Juneau. I got pummeled on the back some more, and more publicity...

Everybody was impressed with my sterling silver Hat-in-the-Ring pin, which had been given to the pilots of our squadron by Eddie Rickenbacker shortly before we left Africa. All of us felt honored to be members of his famous World War I Squadron, and we had done our best to keep up its tradition in World War II, although we had not produced any outstanding flyers like

"Just back from North Africa," this postcard says it all.

61

This photo appeared in the Houston Chronicle. Photo of me and Mr. and Mrs. Sullivan, parents of the five Sullivan Brothers who were lost when the battle cruiser U.S.S. *Juneau* was sunk by the Japanese submarine I-26 on November of 1942 during the Battle of the Coral Sea.

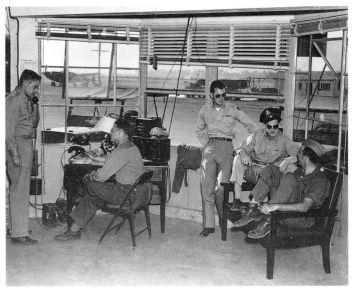

329th Fighter Squadron Operations Office; Santa Ana 1943. Jack Ilfrey sitting on the window ledge.

Rickenbacker. Between Eddie's visit to us in England and his arrival in North Africa, he had had quite a time. When his ship had been lost in the Southwest Pacific, he sat in a life raft for several weeks, but, of course, like the proverbial cat, he had pulled through and was now on his way to Stalingrad on a mission for President Roosevelt.

It was wonderful to get in my car, alone (with Hitler), and drive to Galveston and go swimming. I didn't give a damn if I did ride with Adolph. I figured if the civilians could do it, I had earned the right to follow suit. And it was also a wonderful feeling to be free, knowing you didn't have to get up at dawn and it was comforting to know you would be in the same place at night. The home-cooked meals almost put the powdered eggs and hardtack into limbo—but not quite.

I had not thought much about my nerves until I was home again but I found that automobile horns fairly made me just jump out of my skin. I resented questions, and, above all, I resented the sloppy praise on the bravery of "our boys."

I renewed many old acquaintances, mostly girl friends, as all the boys I had known were off at war. There were plenty of men,

The 329th Fighter Squadron, 332nd Fighter Group, 4th Air Force, Orange County Airport, Santa Ana, California - Summer of 1943. Jack Ilfrey kneeling first on left.

CHAPTER 5: Stateside at Last

Captain Paul Miller, front, Jack Ilfrey, rear, flight instructors, preparing our wives for an illegal "piggy-back" ride in a P-38.

however, at the shipyards who had not yet been drafted and who were having the time of their lives with large overtime earnings. Everyone was prosperous and beer drinking had reached astounding proportions. And while I was in the process of renewing an acquaintance with an old girl friend, we suddenly decided to get married.

We had a very pleasant honeymoon trip out to March Field, California, and up to San Francisco. I was permanently stationed down at the air strip at Santa Ana, where I became a P-38 instructor for replacement pilots. It was now in the early summer of 1943, and the Air Corps was really going in high. One of my old friends, Jack Landers, from Fort Worth, Texas, was at Santa Ana. Jack and I had gone through flying school together and had been buddies at Texas A. & M. Shortly after Pearl Harbor Jack had gone to New Guinea with a P-40 outfit. He had six Jap victories to his credit and had returned to the States about the same time that I landed in Miami. We both had become aces on the same day — 26 December 1942. In another ten months we were to go to England as P-38 squadron commander replacements.

California had changed a great deal. When I was a fresh and green second lieutenant in December '41, the Californians had treated us royally. At that time they were really scared of an invasion and nothing was too good for the comparatively few boys in uniform. I got patted on the back in bars, was treated to drinks, and made to feel like I was destined to be their savior. It was different now. The streets and the bars were swarming with soldiers, sailors, and marines, and the civilians told you about their jobs in the shipyards and war plants, and they no longer bought you drinks. Instead, the serviceman was expected to buy drinks for the civilians. It was a curious change. There was no longer fear of invasion of the West Coast, and with this absence of fear had come not a complete indifference to the men in uniform, but rather a lessening of understanding. The civilians seemed to feel that our pocketbooks were bulging with money, which should have been shared with them.

They forgot a little difference of overtime—P-38 pilots were worth a dime a dozen now in comparison with the few at the time I graduated from flying school.

I had looked forward to having a home in California, but we found it hard to find a place in which to live. We spent several weeks moving from one tourist court to another, and at long last we found a house down on the beach at Balboa, which was near the base at Santa Ana. My landlord made it clear we could not rent any rooms in his 12-room house. Nevertheless, in order to offset the rent of $135 a month, which we could not have afforded, we rented three of the bedrooms to pilots who were stationed at the base with me.

It was a wonderful experience moving into our own house, and we had great fun giving dinners (and trying to cook 'em), and parties, and celebrating at the slightest provocation.

In the Replacement Training Unit at Santa Ana, we taught the boys just out of flying school to fly P-38s, and do formation work. They learned gunnery by shooting at tow targets in the air and also at stationary ground targets. Most of the boys were keen to go overseas, and there were just a few "odd balls." As a rule, we took the wings away from the "odd balls" and gave them an unpleasant ground job, which was good old army policy. I had eight classes in the ten months I stayed at Santa Ana and each class consisted of sixty to a hundred students. Even with twenty-five instructors, I was kept inhumanely busy.

We made every effort to play fair with the boys when requests for overseas duty came through. If headquarters asked us for ten names for South Pacific duty, we would try to find out the boys who wanted to go, and we just didn't arbitrarily submit their names without learning the preference of each man.

Around March 15, '44, Jack Landers, Martin Low, and myself received orders to report to the headquarters of the Eighth Air Force in England as P-38 squadron commander replacements.

On left, Jack Ilfrey during a publicity tour in New York City at the Waldorf Astoria Hotel with Alexander P. de Seversky, founder of the *Seversky Aircraft Corporation***, later to become** *Republic Aircraft***, and General Ralph Royce on right.**

6

BACK TO THE OLD GRIND AGAIN

We reported to the Port of Aerial Embarkation in New York City and the trip overseas this time was a far cry from the epic flight of P-38s in '42. In sixteen hours, or perhaps more, after leaving Manhattan, we were in Scotland, and had made only one stop in Newfoundland for refueling.

At headquarters in London I was assigned to the 79th Fighter Squadron of the Twentieth Fighter Group. The Twentieth was an old prewar West Coast Fighter Group, and it was sorta funny to be in this group now, since my old outfit, the First Fighter Group, had been in keen competition with the Twentieth during maneuvers in Louisiana in the peacetime period of '41.

The Twentieth had really had it rough. They arrived in England during '43 and had pioneered over Germany on long-range escort missions when the Luftwaffe was still strong in numbers and skilled pilots. But now in April '44 we had many more groups in Britain and the Eighth and Ninth Air Force had really been taking care of the Luftwaffe.

It was amazing to me to see the large numbers of P-38s and bombers going to Germany every day. It was still more amazing to see the skill that went into the planning and the execution of these missions—far different from the days in '42 when we would not have dared to use the tactics that were being used now. It was true

Formation of B-17Gs from the 390th Bomb Group. TARGET: GERMANY

Damage to the outer wing of my P-38 MC-O after my head-on collision with a Messerschmitt ME-109.

CHAPTER 6: Back to the Old Grind Again

A testament to the ruggedness of the Lockheed P-38.

Jack Ilfrey, 79th Fighter Squadron, 20th Fighter Group, 8th Air Force, Kingscliffe, England. Spring of 1944.

the Luftwaffe had declined but they were still able to give pretty stiff resistance to our fighters and bombers when they flew over Berlin.

I really had to start all over again. Everything had changed. I had to learn geography anew, the British systems had changed, and

Picadilly Circus - Wartime London - 1944.

strategy was executed with the greatest care for the minutest detail, leaving nothing to chance or error. Long-range flying was something else I had to brush up on but in the end everything turned out to be a breeze.

Things were predominately American now and every square inch of the Isle of Britain was fairly crawling with American bombers, fighters, and troops. You saw more American planes than British and the poor English were really putting up with a hell of a lot of stuff from the Yankees. Our manners were pretty bad.

R. C. Franklin, who had been my instructor at Luke Field, and who had taught me a lot about flying, was the commanding officer of the 79th Squadron. He was soon to finish his tour of duty.

Around the last of April I went on my first mission, flying wing position on Franklin, and we escorted some "heavies" to Hamm, Germany. This was a new kind of combat for me. In North Africa we had operated in small groups, escorting small groups of bombers. Now we were operating in much larger groups, staying together for better protection, and escorting much larger groups of bombers. Also, I was not used to flying such long distances, and being strapped down tight in a fighter for four and a half to five hours at a temperature ranging from 50 to 60 degrees below zero is no frolic. Every detail of the missions was worked down to a science, and the forays were carried out with the utmost precision.

65

My P-38 in the Spring of 1944. Note the long range drop tanks.

79th Fighter Squadron Operations Room.

Control Tower at Kingscliffe - Spring of 1944.

20th Fighter Group Commanding Officers. Left - Col. Harold J. Rau, 20th Fighter Group C.O. - March 20, 1944 to June 25, 1944. Right - Col. Cy Wilson, 20th Fighter Group C.O. - June 25, 1944 to September 27, 1944. Col. Rau became C.O. of the group again on August 27, 1944 until December 18, 1944. Cy Wilson was shot down August 27, 1944. He landed in the North Sea and was taken prisoner. Both are standing in front of Col. Rau's P-38 "Gentle Annie."

On my third mission we escorted the heavy bombers into Berlin, and the very name Berlin had me half-frightened out of my wits. I was leading a flight of four in our squadron of sixteen, and we were up around 30,000 feet, southeast of Berlin, when we were suddenly jumped by a gaggle of 30 to 40 ME-109s. In avoiding the attack, we split up momentarily, and I was forced into a head-on pass with a ME-109. Just after firing I felt a jolt; I looked down and saw an ME-109 spinning down to earth. My own plane was trying to go into a spin, and I was told later by someone who had seen all this action that the ME had come up underneath my plane and had hit my right wing, but at the moment, from where I sat, I could only see that the end of my wing looked like shredded wheat. The collision had ripped open my right wing tank and that engine quit temporarily and threw me into a spin. I left it in a spin for several thousand feet into some clouds and managed to get the conked engine running again by switching gas tanks. I purposely stayed in the clouds to escape detection.

While still in the overcast, I picked up a course that would take me out to the North Sea, as I wanted to get away from the danger in

CHAPTER 6: Back to the Old Grind Again

20th Fighter Group P-38 painted in D-Day Invasion stripes.

Standing in front of my P-38J15LO, #43-8431 coded MC-O. This was my aircraft during D Day Operations.

Captain James "Slick" Morris, 77th F.S. and Col. Barton Russell early C.O. of the 20th Fighter Group. Morris was the first "ace" in the E.T.O. He was shot down July 7, 1944, and was made a P.O.W.

Officer's Club at Kingscliffe. Many nights were spent here!

P-38J10LO "Droop Snoot" showing ten missions symbols on the nose. The name "EZE DOES IT," was given by the lead bombardier of the 20th F.G. Herschel Ezell. He came to the 20th FG after a tour with an 8th Air Force Bomb Group.

the Berlin Area. After flying some minutes on instruments in the overcast, at 15,000 feet, heavy concentrated flak started bursting all around me. Even though I could not be seen, the radar on the heavy anti-aircraft guns was picking me up and directing the fire. Taking evasive action, I started diving down, hoping to break out of the clouds so I could see exactly what I should do. I popped out of the overcast at 7,000 feet and found myself over a large town, which I determined later to be Hamburg. The flak was really snapping at my tail and the only thing that remained for me to do was to dive down as fast as I could and get right on the large river, which appeared to head toward the North Sea. I literally dug furrows in the water and followed the river out to the North Sea and England, some 400 miles away.

I had lost more than a half tank of gas when the ME hit my wing and I had used a lot going full throttle from the center of Hamburg to the North Sea, and I really had to throttle my engines way back in order to have enough fuel to get to England; and even then I sweated it out all the way.

The boys at base had given me up. I was already more than an hour overdue. Upon landing it was found that three to four feet had been knocked off my wing. Even Africa had not been like this, and since my number did not come up that day, I knew it wasn't coming up. For the next few days I laid off. I had no desire to visit Berlin. Adolph could have it as far as I was concerned. But, of course, this was just a passing reaction...

One day I took a plane (a little unofficially) and flew up to see Frank Clark, my old Houston friend, whom I had joined the Air Corps with, and who was now at Goxhill helping to take care of the replacement pilots' pool. Frank had completed a tour of duty in Africa but I never knew he was there until I saw him at Goxhill. I also met a bunch of pilots from my last Santa Ana class, whom I had put on a train in California and waved good-bye to not less than three weeks before. They had just arrived in England by boat and were very much surprised to see me waving hello to them. They did not know I had received my orders just after they left. We had a big beer reunion and several of my ex-students later joined the 79th Squadron.

Major Bob Riemensnider stands in front of his P-38 "Bobby." He was assigned to the 55th Fighter Squadron.

CHAPTER 6: Back to the Old Grind Again

Major R.C. Franklin standing in front of his P-38, "Strictly Stella's Baby." He commanded the 79th Fighter Squadron, and was my instructor at Luke Field.

London Revisited, 1944
My good friend, Jake Gilbertson, and I went on a three-day pass to London. The streets were great masses of G.I.s from all branches of the service and although we didn't know it, this last week in May was to be the last leave the G.I.s would have in a long time, for before two more weeks passed most of them would be either on the Continent or going to the Continent. Jake knew London much better than I did and was able to take me many places I had never heard of. We were definitely not interested in seeing anything historical on this visit. You could thank Africa for our preferring live, warm objects.

I had known the girls of Piccadilly Circus in '42, so I became reacquainted with these Piccadilly "Commandos." They had rightfully earned this nickname because of their approach and tactics, which even to us Americans were tops in brass. The original whores seemed to have organized a young army of their own and prices were higher than ever. In fact, you were often turned down when you didn't offer enough shillings. It was no wonder the term commando stuck to these gals. One of these strumpets approached me one night and asked me if I wouldn't like to go home with her and have a "nice" time. I gave her a quick look and said, before I thought, "Hell, what would be nice about going home with an old bag like you?" I was lucky that night. I didn't get my nose flattened out for making this remark. The Piccadilly "Commandos" were really the last word in brazen hussies...

Jake took me to a place called the American Melody Bar and it turned out to be quite a place, run by quite a woman named Dolores Hunter. Dolores said she came from Boston and claimed to be thirty-five years old, but it was our opinion she'd never see forty-five again. The bright red hair only deceived Dolores herself. She talked like she had been vaccinated with a phonograph needle. She was hep.

The bar was strictly for American combat flyers, and only the boys and gun crews with wings were allowed to enter. Women were taboo. Dolores catered to the bomber crews but we fighter boys gave her a good run for her money. She was one of the out-cussingest, out jokingest women I ever ran across. Regardless, she always had the last word.

Her place always seemed to be open, even for before-breakfast drinks, and Dolores was right there to welcome you in. She had more Scotch than anybody in London, and later on she opened the American Melody Bar (after D day) to all combat men on leave in London—and woe be to any rear-echelon commandos who tried to get in. It was a relief to go into a place like Dolores's bar once in a while where you could be free from dames reaching into your pockets indirectly and also from the strong arm tactics of the Piccadilly "Commandos."

One evening Dolores was telling everybody her thirty-sixth birthday was coming up in a month or two, and since cosmetics were hard to get in England, I thought it would be nice if I presented Dolores with some lipstick, which would go with her red hair. So I wrote my wife accordingly. I never received the lipstick and perhaps my request for a birthday gift for Dolores is one of the reasons why I am enjoying single blessedness today.

We loved to hear Dolores tell about her husbands. We could never determine whether she had had three, four, or five husbands. Some nights when she was mellow, she'd talk about her first husband and from her account, he must had had something on the ball. The only trouble was that he was allergic to work and Dolores had to support both of them.

Dolores was her own bouncer and she was an expert at quieting down the boys when they got too boisterous or started fighting. She rarely ever had to kick anybody out, as her tongue-lashing usually brought apologies and order. But when she did have to kick a G.I. out, he could always come back, if he promised to behave himself.

On the walls of the American Melody Bar were souvenirs from all over the world—all kinds of guns, medals, monies, pictures, and swords. And, speaking of gifts. Dolores really had 'em. Boys, who had returned to London after a leave in the U.S. brought her nylons, costume jewelry, and food delicacies. These remembrances were a tribute to Dolores. She had a quick, warm sympathy, and she took everybody's problem to heart as if it were her own. When-

Captain Merle B. Nichols on the left and Lt. Charles L. Smith. Nichols was a fellow 79th Fighter Squadron pilot. Smith was Squadron Armament Officer.

This photo was taken in the early morning hours of June 6, 1944, the date of the Normandy Invasion. The 20th Fighter Group was assigned to cover the landing beaches.

ever we resented something, Dolores resented it furiously. When we showed anger, Dolores got rip-roaring mad.

She knew where you could get a room for the night, with accommodations to take care of the most exacting situation. When you wanted the best food that London could afford, she'd give you the addresses of black market eating places, and when you got into trouble, you could always telephone Dolores and get the best advice on how to get out of your difficulty. She was a great favorite with all the combat men. We liked her gaiety, her jokes—and her well-supplied stocks of Scotch. I have often wondered what has happened to Dolores and her bar.

We met two well-dressed girls in the swank Park Lane cocktail lounge, and there's something about a cocktail lounge that makes you a little careless. The girls looked attractive in the dim light. After several drinks, they suggested that we take them to the junior officers' mess for dinner. This mess was more or less for the convenience of transient officers and guests. Before going over, however, we took the girls to their flat to change clothes, and, Jake, being a little tight, went into the bathroom instead of the water closet. When one of the girls discovered that Jake was using the douche bowl, you would have thought he had committed a breach of social etiquette. We had used this bowl many times in hotels instead of walking way down to the water closet. Continental bathrooms are more designed to take care of modern woman's needs than the American sandboxes.

When I went up to buy meal tickets in the mess, the girl at the cashier's desk said to me; "Where did you get those two? They're in here every night for a good meal, with two different officers. They never come in with the same men." And I said, sort of feeling my drinks and being in an obliging mood, "Well, do you want us to fix it so that they won't come back in here again?" The cashier said, "That'll be wonderful. How will you do it?" And I said, "Well, we'll be real boisterous and we'll insult the girls. We'll show all kinds of bad manners, and after a few minutes of this tell the manager to come over and tell the girls if they can't find two better officers than those rowdy so-called officers to bring in here, to please not come back." She said, "O.K. I will." When we got seated at the table, I went into my act. Jake caught on at once and started doing his part. We talked loud, laughed hysterically, overturned the water and broke a cup, called the girls "old bags" (which they were), and in general displayed the worst in manners. The poor girls tried to quiet us, saying if we didn't stop they'd never be allowed in the mess again, and this caused us to redouble our efforts and brought on wilder hysterics. It also brought the manager over to our table and he told the girls the mess could not have officers like us in the place, and since they were more or less responsible for our being

CHAPTER 6: Back to the Old Grind Again

Lt. Art Heiden shaking hands with his Crew Chief after a victory.

Tony LeVier on a visit to Kingscliffe. Seen here in front of his P-38J10LO, "Snafuperman." He was a Lockheed Test Pilot. Spring of 1944.

there that when the meal was finished to please not come back again. As the manager turned away, he gave us a knowing wink. The poor girls gulped down their food and hurried out. I kinda felt sorry for them. It was pretty hard for some Britons to get a good meal.

The Neptune Plan
Things were beginning to get tight about this time. There was a tenseness in the air and we knew something was coming up but we didn't know exactly what. On missions into France we had noticed large concentrations of boats in the southern English ports, and on the third of June our base was closed, all leaves and furloughs canceled. We received orders and instructions on how to paint large black and white stripes on the wings and fuselages of our airplanes.

The C.O. of our group got us all together on the night of June 4, and said, "This is it," and proceeded to explain the instructions he had received from higher headquarters as to the part we would

The 20th Fighter Group in formation during D-Day Operations.

Captain George Weymms, 20th FG Operations Officer.

play in the Neptune Plan, D day. Zero hour was to be early in the morning of June 6. Squadrons of P-38's were to cover the boats because the Lightnings were easily recognized. We actually started patrolling on D-Day minus one, at which time large concentrations of boats were converging from every port in southern England. All that day and for a couple of days previous, the heavy bombers had been blasting the French coast very heavily between the area of Boulogne and Le Treport. This bombing was to mislead the enemy. The Normandy Coast, where the actual landings were made, was not heavily bombed until a few hours before zero hour. On D day our mission took off at 5:00 A.M.

When daylight broke, we had a "command performance" view of the invasion scene. It was a sight I shall never forget—four thousand boats merged into one, big, spectacular prong, ready to lash itself on the enemy coast, thousands of men lying flat on their stomachs in the boats, and hundred of airplanes patrolling the sixty-mile stretch from the English coast to Normandy. It was cold and clammy that morning and I felt sorry for the boys in the boats below.

Hitler would have needed several atomic bombs to have stopped this big prong, and even then I don't see how it would have been possible for him to have dropped bombs on the boats, as we had an air screen over the ships that was almost impregnable.

I flew for ten hours that day, broken up into three stretches. The Luftwaffe remained in hiding. During the few previous months we had made a determined effort to destroy German fighters, strafing them on the ground and shooting them in the air.

The air screen was kept over the shipping area and invaded beaches for a week or more, during which time the Luftwaffe didn't put in much of an appearance. Our troops had firmly established a large beach head and already several fighter strips were in operation by P-47s of the Ninth Air Force. We in the P-38's were taken off patrol duty and started to ground strafe and dive bomb again, along with escorting the heavies into France and Germany.

D day plus six was my fateful day. It finally happened to me, too. . .

Captain Lindol Graham. The 79th Fighter Squadron's first "ace." He was later killed in action.

7

"IT FINALLY HAPPENED TO ME, TOO..."

All of us fighter pilots had said it couldn't happen to us. "I'm too damn good to get shot down", but deep down in our minds I think we all had a plan as to what we would do if it ever did happen.

It was ironic, just before takeoff late that afternoon, the way I had briefed my squadron. I had told the boys it was my opinion from now on that if anyone was shot down in France, the best thing to do would be to lie low and try to find a hiding place with some French family until the allies moved into their section or to possibly work up toward the front lines.

Since the afternoon and evening of June 5th the 20th Gp. had been covering the invasion in our easily recognizable P38 Lightnings. At Zero hour, 0756 June 6th we had a ringside "command performance" view of the invasion. A sight we will never forget.

By June 11th, Hitler's vaunted Atlantic Wall had been cracked wide open and a great allied army was firmly established on the Normandy coast. The 20th was taken off patrol and assigned dive bombing and strafing mission targets behind the lines.

Our mission this day was to dive bomb the railroad bridge over the Loire River at LaPossiniere not far from the city of Angers.

Our P38s were loaded with two 1000 pounders and I led 16 ships of the 79th Sq. We took off at 1848 and arrived in the target area at 2030. We came in out of the west with the sun on our backs and successfully dive bombed the bridge. Several direct hits severed the tracks and inflicted serious damage on the bridge structure. We were then to strafe rail and motor traffic and any other targets of opportunity from the Loire, north into Normandy.

We had just reassembled at about 8,000 feet when I spied a locomotive with steam up in the village of LeLion just north of Angers. The Germans had become pretty wise to our attacks on trains and usually had several flak cars on the trains, especially one behind the engine; therefore, in order to do a complete job of knocking out the locomotives, we planned coordinated attacks on them. The leader, as a rule, went after the engine while his wing man went in after the guns on the flak car, and the others in the squadron provided cover.

I dived down towards the engine, and while taking aim at it, caught a glimpse, out of the corner of my eye, at some tracer bullets

My crew and I standing in front of my P-38. I owe much of my success to all of them. We were a team, they kept me flying.

"In the Office." The cockpit of a P-38 was very difficult to bail out of. Normal procedure was to open the top hatch of the canopy, roll the side windows down, and roll over the aircraft and fall out!

My evasion photo. Taken in England 1944. This photograph was a part of a combat pilot's escape kit along with food, maps, money, etc. It was to be used for forged ID papers to fool the Germans.

coming up at me from the flak car behind the engine. Just after I opened up on the locomotive I saw the boiler explode and pulled up, my whole right engine burst into flame and smoke and somebody yelled over the radio "Bail out Jack; you're on fire." My cockpit immediately filled with smoke, blinding and choking me. I jettisoned my canopy and the smoke cleared momentarily, and I could tell I certainly wasn't very high above the ground. However, without any hesitation, I released my safety belt and shoulder harness and went over the left side, opening the parachute immediately. I had just looked up and yelled "that S.O.B. works", when I hit the corner of a farm house and bounced off into the yard.

Jesse Carpenter, a pilot who was with me that day described it years later, "a horrible scene when the flak got you the day you strafed the train and your right engine torched - and your chute popped - oscillated once before you hit the corner of that French building - too damned close, Jack".

Art Heiden, another pilot on that mission, said there were some camouflaged 88's, field artillery guns in a field right next to the village and as I flew over this field, going in for the kill of the locomotive, they were just snapping at my ass.

He looked around for a field to land in so he could pick me up, but too many trees and glider barriers were erected in cleared spots. Now this is total camaraderie - a bond that existed between combat fighter pilots that few people can attain in a lifetime.

So there I was - one minute, the sound of guns, the roar of engines, the smell of smoke, the touch of fire and rush of air as my body hurtled through it. Then the jolt of stopping in mid air, complete silence and laying flat on the ground in enemy occupied territory.

We pilots used to kiddingly joke with each other about a "Pucker Factor" scale of from one to 10. I had just hit the ultimate - No. 10.

In a matter of seconds I was up on my feet and determined that physically I was still in one piece . . . threw off my parachute harness and dinghy and saw that the parachute canopy had fallen across the roof of the house - so not wanting it to be a beacon for the Germans I pulled it off and wadded it into a pile - then threw off my helmet, oxygen mask and goggles, Mae West and heavy flying boots. Meanwhile, during all this a man with a pitch fork in his hand came out of a barn across the yard and 3 children appeared. They all stood watching me. Without thinking about it I asked the direction north and the man pointed. I grabbed my escape and first-aid kits attached to the chute and tore off through the woods in the direction the man had pointed. By this time I could see the smoke from my crashed and burning P38 and hear the ammunition exploding. I wanted to make tracks out of the vicinity. I ran through trees, over, under and through hedgerows until exhausted and fell into some tall grass.

I now had to urinate in the worst way but could not, as I was still registering too high on the Pucker Factor Scale.

I got out my rubberized waterproof map and determined my position to be about 10 miles northwest of Angers, deep inside German territory.

Thinking of what I had told my squadron several hours before, I decided to get farther away from where I was shot down and try to find a place to hide.

Jean Voileau, the young Frenchman that I first met, he greatly aided me in starting my evasion.

CHAPTER 7: "It Finally Happened to Me, Too..."

Odette Charvau, 1944.

I dismissed entirely the idea of heading south and across the Pyrenees Mountains into Spain, which had been the accustomed route of airmen who made their escape before the allied invasion.

I took off my flying suit, insignia and tie. That left me dressed in a gray sweater, shirt with open neck, no insignia, a pair of green O.D. trousers and G.I. shoes. I put all items from my escape and first-aid kits in my pockets and tried to relax in the grass. In a short while it became dusk, at which time I got out on a small country road and started walking north.

In a few minutes two boys on bicycles approached me from the rear and one of them rode right up to me and asked in very broken English if I was the American "aviateur" who had jumped out of a Lightning earlier. Sensing he was friendly and having nothing to lose one way or another, because of the way I was dressed and knowing very little French, I told him I was.

He smiled and said that he and his friend had just come from the wreckage of my P38 and that the Germans were in the neighborhood looking for me.

He asked me to come with them to their village and he would see about hiding me. He pumped me on the bicycle and after a little while I let him ride while I pumped the bicycle.

It was after dark when we got to the village of Andigne and he asked me to hide on the side of the road while he and his friend Raymond went to see what might be arranged. My young friend was named Jean, 17 years old. Raymond was 19 and lived with his sister Odette and father, who ran a cafe and bar in the village. Jean and his family lived next door to the cafe.

After a short while they came back and took me to the cafe, which had living quarters upstairs. I met everyone and we sat down over wine, bread and a hastily prepared dish for me.

Jean was the only one who spoke any English, but as they talked about my staying there I could gather that the father seemed somewhat against it because of a few German soldiers who came into the cafe from time to time. But Odette pointed out there were no Germans stationed in the area and the chances of my being discovered were very remote.

After a long discussion and much hesitation the family agreed that, even at great risk to themselves, I could stay with them until liberated by the allies in the north which we all knew would take place sooner or later though the father had heard the Germans say they were *"driving them back into the sea"*. We all lifted our glasses and said *"A Votre Sante"* and went to bed. I shared the one with Raymond.

It had been a hectic day for me and I had the feeling that God had been holding my hand.

When I went down to the kitchen next morning, it was quite a surprise to see these people seemed to have plenty of foods, chickens, eggs, milk, butter and some fresh fruit. We very seldom saw these in England. However, they lacked such things as coffee, salt and sugar. The kitchen, with it's big table in the middle, served as the family living and dining area and the rest of the downstairs was given over to the cafe. Just off to one side of the kitchen was the cellar which was well-stocked with the wines they had made. There was no running water and all water had to be carried from the well in the village square a half a block away.

The whole family made every effort to please me and were eager to talk. The limited French I had picked up in North Africa seemed to be of no use to me, but when Jean was there we were able to understand one another, and when he was away at school the English-French dictionary that he found for me was a great help in trying to talk with the girls. There was another girl who came and helped out in the cafe during the day. It didn't take much doing to pick up a little kitchen lingo. Whenever Odette wanted wood for the stove she would just point to the stove. If she wanted the floor swept she'd point to the broom. Then with the dictionary we could make conversation out of one word or I would say one word sentences.

My first paralyzing fear of the Germans was partly overcome by watching them through the window when they passed on the road in front of the cafe and while I was never allowed in the cafe when customers were present, once I happened to be sweeping up the floor when some young German soldiers came in for a drink of cool wine. I immediately started sweeping toward the back and right into the kitchen and hoped the Germans hadn't noticed my casual but none-the-less hurried retreat.

The Jerries laughed a great deal and looked more like Boy Scouts than soldiers. Whenever the Germans came in I got a signal from Odette and dashed for the cellar. She said the enemy had never tried to take anything away from them and that they always paid for their drinks.

She kept me busy, chopping wood, washing dishes, sweeping floors, even tried my hand at cooking, however, more wine was served in the cafe than food.

The electricity came on two or three times for five or ten minutes each day and whenever it did I'd make a mad dash for the radio to tune in on the BBC in hope of catching the English news. At other times they would listen to the French news, broadcast by the Germans.

After supper we'd gather around the big table in the kitchen, drink wine and play records on an ancient victrola. The well-used needles scratched out "Flatfoot Floogie," "Tuxedo Junction" and assorted French tunes. Scratching or no scratching the music was good to hear and we would have done a little dancing if there would have been room in the kitchen.

These evenings brought on a bombardment of questions about America. Example, when I told them my father was a banker and that I had an automobile back home they wanted to know if I, too, were rich like the Americans they had seen in movies. They did not fully understand when I explained that I was not rich; that when I was commissioned a 2nd Lt. in 1941, my base pay was $125.00 per month plus $75.00 for flight pay and that it was very easy to trade in my 1937 LaSalle, which I had just finished paying for, for a new 1941 Mercury and come out with $27.50 per month payments. No problem, those car dealers and finance companies were glad to see us.

The villagers would come into the cafe at night to talk over the war situation with the family, and I met a number of the trustworthy ones.

After a few days however, the family became worried over the fact that word had spread around that I, an American aviator, was being hidden by them. At that time I did not fully realize the extent these wonderful French people were putting themselves in jeopardy with their German captors.

In any event I had been piecing together the news broadcasts that I was able to hear and had come to the conclusion that the allies were bogged down on the Normandy front and it looked like they were going to stay put for awhile. Plus, the fact the family was telling me the French news, which of course was put out by the Germans, were claiming to be driving the allies back into the sea.

So I made up my mind that I'd better try to get the hell up there before it became another Dunkirk.

I approached the family with my ideas. Could they give me one of their bicycles and some French clothing as I wanted to try to make the journey up to and possibly across the front lines. At first they balked, but then after talking it over thoroughly it was decided that Jean could get me a French identity card from the town hall, as all Frenchmen were registered with the Germans. I had several pictures of myself taken in civilian clothing in my escape kit which worked fine on the identity card. Jean took my first name and Robert's and called me Jacques Robert (Jack Roberts), cultivateur (farmer); my age, height and weight were given and under remarks he put that I had been injured due to bombings in Angers and was deaf.

Odette obligingly said I could have her bicycle.

In discussing the route I should take we decided it best for me to take the main road north, N162, to Caen which at the time was being besieged by the British.

I sat down and completely memorized my set of maps and some French maps that Jean provided me. The roads I was to take, towns I was to pass through and distances interpolated into kilometers. The father and the boys gave me many hints and pointers. I was now able to say many phrases in French, ask for food and water, directions, greet people, etc.

I gave them all the money in my escape kit, which included American dollars and gold coins, English pounds, Belgian and French francs, German marks, Dutch guilders and Spanish pesetas.

They laughed at my crisp new looking franc notes saying they had not seen any of these in several years and in turn provided me with a few worn franc notes and some bread coupons to help me on my journey.

Odette composed a note in French that read something like this: To Whom It May Concern: This boy, Jacques Robert, from Angers, is trying to get to Bayeux (which was in American hands) to see his parents. He has been injured in a bombing raid and is deaf and cannot speak. Please let him pass. Dr. R. Armand.

We all got up early the morning I left and Odette fixed me a good breakfast and prepared some chicken, bread and butter in a small canvas bag to tie to the bicycle, including the inevitable bottle of wine.

I was dressed in Robert's black beret, pants and coat, Odette's green shirt and a pair of Jean's old shoes. I had nothing on me which would identify me as an American or British in the event I was searched. Not even my dog tags, which I later caught hell about from American intelligence in London. Jean gave me a pocket knife and a few matches. I felt confident I would make the trip.

With much embracing and kissing from the entire family, I departed at daybreak with bon voyages echoing in my ears.

As I pedaled away from the village in the cool, crisp morning, it was good to be out-of-doors again and I fairly lapped up the fresh air and longed for a cup of coffee and a cigarette.

Raymond Charvau, 1944.

CHAPTER 7: "It Finally Happened to Me, Too..."

After going about five kilometers I reached the main road, N162, which was to take me north, and up to this time I had not seen anyone on the road. I looked up and down the road and a short distance to the south, towards Angers, I saw three parked German trucks and some soldiers and was relieved I didn't have to go that way. This observation was soon to be of use because after a few more kilometers I came upon a lone parked German truck.

Literally shaking in my boots I managed to pedal on, but just as I came along side the truck a German soldier jumped out of the truck and started yelling at me in German. I thought sure as hell this was it and was ready to surrender. But it didn't prove to be that serious. I had enough presence of mind to realize he wanted to know if I had seen two or three trucks back down the road, I answered, "Oui, Monsieur." He got back into the truck and I continued on with renewed confidence. Here was the first German I had seen at close range. He had spoken to me and I hadn't died yet.

The French countryside looked very peaceful in the early morning. Some of the farms along the road were beginning to wake up. The men and boys seemed to have no modesty when it came to relieving themselves in the front yard, against the houses or trees. The women would come to the door with the slop jar and just toss it out.

I passed through several small villages, not seeing much of anything along the road and around mid-morning came to Chateau Gontier, my first large town. I was first impressed with the friendliness of the people, walking or bicycling in the streets. Everyone had a "Bon jour, Monsieur" to say and I would mostly just nod back, hoping this wasn't too American. I did notice some damage along the railroad tracks which I presumed were leading towards the railway station. Men were working on the tracks and I did see one shot up boxcar. The rest of my passing through the town was uneventful and I hit the countryside again. About noon I picked out a nice spot off the road and sat down to eat my chicken. While I was eating I saw some German trucks loaded with soldiers go by. The trucks were highly camouflaged with tree limbs and branches.

After resting and drinking my wine, which did not quench my thirst, I started out again and knew I was going to have to find some water to drink very soon.

I spied a farmhouse off the road with a woman working in the front yard. I rode up and asked her in my best French for a drink of water, but she, evidently seeing I was a traveler insisted on my having wine, but I insisted on H_2O and she pointed to a well and I went and got myself a drink, hoping my typhoid shots would take care of me.

I saw many Germans and much equipment off and on the road that afternoon. The Jerries didn't seem to bother the French and the French stayed away from the Germans. There were refugees on the road on bicycles and in carts and I looked just like one of them, even though most of them were going south but I was going north.

I was still in fairly flat country and the going was easy - easier than the next few days proved to be. Even with frequent rests, this first day was getting rugged.

I was making very good time down a small grade into the town of Laval when I suddenly noticed that the main road I was on was going to pass through the outer perimeter of an airdrome and before I knew it I was right upon a sentry gate and a German soldier had stepped out to stop me. I decided it was too late and would look suspicious to turn around, so, gathering all my wits I rode straight up to the sentry and stopped. He spoke to me in French and wanted to know where I was going and wanted to see my identification.

I had to play my deaf act here because it would have been a dead give-away if I had tried to speak French to him. I put over that I was deaf, "sourd," with hand motions and showed him my identity card, which I hoped didn't look too new. He shook his head and said "nein," stepped into his booth and punched a buzzer. I knew for sure the game was up now. A German officer appeared from a building next to the road and the two were talking in German as they came up to me. I handed the officer my note from the doctor. He read it and it seemed to satisfy him and he passed it back to me with a wave-on signal. However, the other sentry was still holding my identity card and being afraid to speak, I politely reached out and took it out of his hand, putting both documents in my jacket pocket. Trying not to faint I was able to get back on my bicycle quickly and shoved off.

I rode right through the airdrome and saw what was left of the installations. Most of the buildings and hangars were on the ground and I took pride in the fact that I had dive-bombed this airdrome and had contributed to some of the wreckage. I saw two wrecked P38's and wondered what had happened to the pilots, and there were also several of our external belly tanks laying around.

In a very camouflaged revetment under some trees, not over 100' off my road, were several Messerschmitt 109's being warmed up as if preparing for a flight. I pedaled slowly, looking, and it brought to my mind the time in North Africa, over a year and half ago, that I had flown one of these at Biskra which had been left behind by the Germans when we took over the airfield there. One of our Sgt. crew chief mechanics, who knew German, had carefully tuned it back to good flying condition and over all the instruments and flying controls had written in English on adhesive tape the proper names of each, gas R.P.M., air speed, etc. It was on a dare that I took it up, however, came time to land, I quite suddenly discovered that neither the Sgt. nor I had ever mentioned or adhesive marked the flaps control. I had one hell of a time getting that mean little s.o.b. back on the ground.

With these thoughts in mind there was a fleeting moment that— maybe I could do it again? But these 'illusions of grandeur' left as quickly as they had come up, and I pedaled on.

The Germans had quite a contingent of French laborers working on the field, but I continued right through, past the sentry box on the other end without being molested and then on in to Laval.

And here I saw my first big damage from American bombers. The railroad station and yards and surrounding blocks of houses were destroyed. There were a lot of Germans in town, including women who were the equivalent of our WACS.

It was almost dark when I got through the town and knowing the Germans had a curfew on the French from sunrise to daybreak, and also being tired, hungry and thirsty I started looking for a place to spend the night. I saw a barn way off to itself in the corner of a field and went over to it.

Inside the barn was a nice sandy dirt floor, which felt pretty good when I fell down on it. I ate the rest of my food and drank what little wine was left, but I had to go without water. Sleep was not to be far off but it started to get real cool. There was a two-wheel dray in the barn with a canvas top on it, so with my little boy scout knife that Jean had given me I cut out the canvas top and covered up with it. Poor Frenchman...at least he had donated to the allied cause.

I slept soundly and awoke with the chickens. My legs felt stiff and sore but otherwise I was greatly refreshed. When I pushed my bicycle out to the road I discovered I had a flat tire on the front wheel. I sat down feeling disgusted and at a loss as to what to do. It wasn't long, however, until a priest, dressed in his black robe and funny hat, came by on a bicycle and stopped, asking if he could be of assistance. I felt safe in telling him I was an American trying to make my way up through the lines. He was amazed at first and then in good English told me to follow him to his parish about three miles up the road and that he would fix my tire and give me something to eat. He got off his bicycle and we both pushed our wheels and talked all the way to his church.

His fellow priest prepared a very good meal for me which I ate heartily and after some tea and cognac I felt invigorated. I had never been an agnostic nor had I ever been a Catholic but these young fellows in this, what turned out to be a seminary, treated me like royalty. I spent the rest of the day and that night with them. Most of them spoke, at least, some English and continually asked me all kinds of questions about the U.S., how the war was going, and couldn't get over the fact that I was an ace (killer, one said) fighter pilot. Although I didn't feel like a killer, I suppose you could say we fighter pilots had a license to kill. My only thought was to get that s.o.b. before he got me.

In any event a good time was had by all. They had been hoarding things since before the war and for the occasion brought out Early Times, Lucky Strikes, (before the green went to war), German chocolate yet, and Green River. If memory serves me, that was what we used to buy in high school, shortly after prohibition, for 99 cents a fifth, or was it a pint. I can hazily remember them throwing me into a feather mattress bed like I had never experienced in South Texas, that folded up around me and I went off into blissful dreams, oblivious to the war around me.

Next morning, back to reality, hang-over and all, hearty breakfast, tire repaired on the bicycle, I'm somewhat thinking I might like to stay here in this Utopia until the glorious allies come through the area.

But a priest came pedaling up the driveway and the others told me he's very Anti-American and I should get going right away. It seemed the Americans had bombed him out of his church and killed many of his parishioners and friends in Laval. So with my canvas bag filled with more food and water this time, I took off.

I pedaled on north for awhile without much difficulty until I came to a blockade in the road. A German sentry asked for my identity card, looked me and my knapsack over thoroughly and let me through. I had been told that I would probably run across these blockades and that they were nothing to be afraid of.

In the early afternoon I reached the town of Mayenne and went through it without incident, seeing very little damage. The road I was on followed a pretty little river and at a secluded spot off the road I decided to take a much needed overall bath, as I hadn't had one since before leaving England that afternoon of my uncompleted mission, although at the moment I was working hard to complete it.

I was living from minute to minute, knowing only the events which were behind me and being unable to foretell what was ahead. I stripped to my birthday suit and plunged into the cool water. It felt wonderful. While I was using some of the sand as a substitute for soap, I looked up and saw two French boys on the bank where my bicycle and clothes were, staring at me. Both of them appeared to be in their late teens or early twenties and one spoke to me but I didn't understand what he said. When I started swimming toward them, the boy spoke again and when I did not reply he got angry and talked louder. Having no clothes on I stayed down in the water, sorta sweating out what was going to come next. Then finally I got the idea they wanted to know what I was doing there and it came to the point where I had to talk, or do something. So with gestures and a few words in French I told them I was deaf. I climbed out and brushed the water off me as I was going to put my clothes on over a wet body. The boy who had been doing all the talking threw me a rag he had and gave me a friendly smile.

I felt relieved and reached into my bag and pulled out the food and the few remaining cigarettes the priests had given me and offered them some. They both immediately took a cigarette and while I was putting on my clothes tried to engage in conversation through gestures. I was now convinced that they were good boys so I told them in my best French I was an American aviator on my way to join the allies. This brought on exclamations of surprise and the one who had done all the previous talking burst out in almost perfect English, "Why didn't you tell us? You had us fooled. We thought you might just be up to no good and we were only interested in seeing that you didn't get too far on our property and steal something from us."

They invited me to their home and upon our arrival there, immediately opened a bottle of Calvados. We later named this, American Anti-Freeze. The two boys were brothers and the older one who spoke fair English had been in Canada and U.S. before the war visiting relatives and friends. We seemed to have a lot in common and talked about everything.

They thought my plan was a good one but wanted me to stay with them for a while. I gratefully accepted their offer of food and a bed for the night. We arose early the next morning and even though I had a Calvados headache my confidence and morale were way up.

I bade farewell to my friends on the little farm by the river near Ambrieres.

Now I began to hit the hilly rolling countryside of Normandy and, oh, how I did cuss those hills if I pushed that bicycle up a hill once, I did it a thousand times, each time falling on it and coasting swiftly to the bottom, only to start all over again. All of my previous thoughts of a bicycle trip through Europe were now leaving my head. But I'd be thankful that I did have this bicyclette.

CHAPTER 7: "It Finally Happened to Me, Too..."

The cafe that I stayed in during my first few days of evasion. The photo was taken on my return visit to the area in 1983.

All in all I did pretty well that day. During mid-morning I had sort of been playing tag with a convoy of six trucks full of Nazi youths. None of them appeared to be over seventeen or eighteen years old. The trucks were moving slowly and would stop very often. Once, after passing each other three or four times, the soldiers motioned for me to hang on if I wanted to, and as tired as I was, I did. The Germans said nothing to me but they were all laughing and talking just like any group of teenagers anywhere.

We had covered a few more miles when a flight of six P38's appeared and, brother; did those Germans stop and get out of the trucks in a hurry. I pedaled on for all I was worth. The Lightnings spotted the trucks, in spite of the fact that the vehicles were highly camouflaged with leaves and branches, and echeloned for attack.

I got up to the top of the next hill and watched the fighters ground strafe the hell out of the trucks. It was a very exhilarating experience for me and I felt like jumping up and down, clapping and screaming approval. They set all of them on fire. But it did mean I was without a lift.

It was beautiful country in this part of France. The road was still following a river and there were only occasional Germans and equipment to mar the beauty of the scene.

At one point in the river several soldiers, the priests, my swimming companions, and others had said one of my greatest dangers would be that the Germans would probably take my bicycle away from me.

As I neared Domfront a lone German soldier walking in the opposite direction stopped me and demanded my bicycle. I put a determined fight to keep it by telling him my "mama" and my "papa" lived down the road quite a piece and I had to get there.

My getting home didn't make any difference to the Nazi and I was just going to get off the bicycle when a truck came down the road going his way. I pointed to it and he flagged it down and got in. I was saved again, by what, I don't know.

I went on through Domfront, which had been pretty badly damaged by the allied bombers, and when I got on the other side of the town a truckload of Germans stopped and asked me for directions to someplace I didn't know and I just pointed and they tore off. Lucky again.

Toward late afternoon I approached the town of Flers, which appeared to be a very beautiful place, sitting upon a hill. Everything was pretty and green and large open valleys were all around. I heard a large group of bombers in the distance and knew by the sound that they were B-17's.

I sat down to rest and watch the show. I had not waited long until the bombers, escorted by P38's, most likely some from my own Ftr. Gp., came right to the town of Flers and bombed the railroad yards. Flers was an important railroad junction, and while I had been working my way out of occupied France, our American 8th Air Force fighters and bombers out of England had been bombing and strafing every military target they could find to allow the allied ground forces to advance.

It was a beautiful sight to me, not to the French, I'm sure, to watch the B-17's roll in and drop their bombs. I was only several miles out of the city on a hill looking down on the spectacle. As far away as I was the ground trembled from the impact of the bombs.

After the planes left the whole center of the town was a maze of dust, fire and smoke, which rose several thousand feet above the city. I could have taken some wonderfully revealing pictures of what a bombing means if I had only had a camera. French civilians had not seen cameras or film for several years.

There was no doubt on this raid that bombers were supposed to bomb only the railroad yards, but it was impossible to concentrate on so small a target from such a high altitude that the bombers had to fly, and I was soon to see, at a very first-hand view, that even though the bombs had hit the railroad yards, many bombs had hit long or short and crashed into the buildings surrounding the yards, causing destruction and fires. The streets were full of rubble, lots of it from previous bombings.

After having pushed my bicycle over piles of rubble I was able to get back to the main road on the other side of Flers and it was time for me to start thinking again about looking for a place to stay. For several days now I had been doing this and felt like an old hand at it. I was beginning to hear the guns on the front and a new sort of feeling came over me. Was I to complete this mission at last? And even though I still had thirty or so miles to go, hearing the guns made it seem closer.

I saw two old ladies in a farmyard and I went up and asked them for food and drink. When they hesitated, I pulled out a few of my French francs and offered to pay. I suddenly realized that in almost 200 miles of travel I had not spent a franc. The old ladies still hesitated so I pulled out a few of the bread ration coupons I had never used and that turned the trick.

They took me into the dirt floor kitchen where chickens were roaming around at will and cooked up some eggs, potatoes and meat. I couldn't tell what kind of meat but I ate it along with the wine offered me and it was good. One of the old ladies indicated I could sleep in the barn but I didn't know whether to trust them or not, however, being a light sleeper I figured I could hear if anything out of the ordinary took place. Hell, I slept like a log on the hay and even the bugs in it didn't bother me until the first crow, which was practically in my ear.

While I was washing my face and drinking some cool well water one of the old gals came to the back door and said she had something to eat for me. It turned out to be more eggs and some sort of hot chocolate drink that was rather tasty. It helped out, did the trick, and all I had to use was a well worn franc note. I thanked the old ladies in my best French, gave them a few of those franc notes, the chickens were now devouring the one I had used, and departed to the north. I was always traveling towards the north. My memory was beginning to fail somewhat but I finally remembered that Conde' was the next largest town up from Flers. I was seeing more refugees heading south, German trucks and equipment moving north. I didn't bother anyone and no one bothered me. I reached Conde' at an estimated noon time. I knew I was getting closer and closer to the front, but didn't have any idea what I would do once I did get there. I could only imagine, that this time it wouldn't be or look anything like "All Quiet on the Western Front."

It took me a couple of hours to get through Conde', or I should say over Conde', as most of this town was one big mass of rubble. The bombers had really done a job here. Instead of streets, there were just lanes several feet deep in toppled buildings, and now and then there was a gaping hole where a bomb had spread the rubble.

A river ran through the town and for a moment I didn't know how I was going to get across as there were no bridges left standing. I saw dead cows and other livestock floating in the river and a couple of bloated human bodies and wondered what had happened to all the rest of the people. No one was stirring and it was ghostly quiet. A few small fires and smoke were coming from some of the rubble around me. I finally found a piece of the under structure of a bridge that still stretched erratically across the river and I inched my way over to the other side.

It was hard to decide which way to go but my fighter pilot training and combat flying had instilled a sixth sense, of sorts, as to directions and I instinctually knew which way to go north towards Caen. I had to carry my bicycle over long blocks of knocked out buildings and strewn rubble. I gradually worked out toward the residential section, which was not so badly damaged, and the streets were passable. I pedaled on in to open country and was able to make better time.

There were many more Germans now and a lot of equipment. Communications men were busy stringing wires. I noticed there were yellow, red and blue wires. I pedaled and pedaled and was feeling somewhat oblivious to the war going on around me and middle to late afternoon I approached Thury-Harcourt.

I was beginning to see large guns, the infamous 88's in position in the fields, all expertly camouflaged. At this point I became undecided as to whether to try going on to Caen or not. It was not too very far off and I didn't know who held it, British, Americans or German, so I turned northwest toward Bayeux relying on my note from the doctor and the fact that it had, at least earlier, been in American hands.

In a round about way, again relying on my directions instinct, I pedaled into the village of Erecy. Dead cows and horses were lying around and I could hear the whizz and explosions of shells from the long-range allied guns. I still didn't know whether I was in front of American or British troops.

While I was at the village well in the square, drinking and filling my bottle with water, a young boy came up and asked me a question I didn't understand. He repeated the question and I caught something about my being a stranger and where was I going. I replied "Bayeux." He started shaking his head no, and again I caught the words 'Yanks and Tommys'.

It was easy to see this village was in German hands because of all the feverish activity that was taking place. Several Frenchmen stood around looking unconcerned and the kid seemed just as detached as the others. But I took a chance with him and told him I was hungry. He asked me to follow him to his house on the outskirts of the village. His mother and sister made me welcome and the first thing they did was show me an American and British flag.

I gathered from what I could make out from the conversation they were preparing for the liberation by the allies and were very much enthused. When I told them I was an American "aviateur" there was much embracing and kissing, in the good old French manner.

It developed the mother had lived in Maryland, right out of Baltimore, for several years before the war and she spoke fair to good English. The daughter brought out wine and in addition to the usual eggs, she fixed some cabbage and something that resembled sweet potatoes, and some goat meat. We had a celebration that night, although we had to keep quiet as we didn't want to arouse the suspicions of the Germans. Friends came in, mostly young people around the age of the girl and myself and it was interesting to talk with them, mostly through the mother. I learned how the occupation had been, the shortages of everything, what they thought of the Germans, however, I'm sure the mother didn't translate all the cuss words.

We could hear the whine of the shells before they hit and the noise didn't seem to bother these Frenchmen; but it sure bothered the hell out of me. One man reported that he had learned Caen had been under a terrific siege, very bad destruction, but should be in British hands by now. He also thought the Americans held Bayeux and that the only thing holding up the allied advance were the Jerry's big guns. They seemed to think that if I just went on up the road I was on I should eventually make contact with the British or possibly the Americans. Good for them, I thought, but the mother didn't translate any percentages to me of my making it.

Around dusk, after 10 p.m. they prepared to retire. The mother said I could sleep with the boy but that we should all leave our clothes and shoes on in case we had to make a hasty exit. Some sleep! About the time I'd get to sleep the big guns would start firing and I'd keep listening for the one with my name on it. Daybreak came, none too soon, and I did feel better after splashing cold water on my face. The mother made some much hoarded coffee and liberally fortified mine with Calvados, that good old American anti-freeze, that put a charge in my stomach and confidence in my mind.

The road out of the village was a small narrow winding one bordered by hedgerows and trees, and it was filled with branches

CHAPTER 7: "It Finally Happened to Me, Too..."

and leaves which the shells had knocked off the trees. Shells from both British and German guns were whizzing over my head. So this is no-man's land, I thought. Most uncomfortable feeling.

Riding was hard and I was doing more pushing than riding. A little more Calvados and I exhilarated on.

Shortly before reaching Fontenay I ran head on into two young German soldiers who were carrying one of their wounded comrades. Their eyes lighted on my bicycle and I could see the "mama-papa" act wouldn't work, so when they demanded the bike to put the wounded boy on, I got off and let them have it at once. Thank you, Odette, for a very lovely trip. However, before letting me leave one of them frisked me thoroughly and came out with the knife Jean had given me. He also put one hand inside my shirt, at the neck, and felt under my arms. If I had been wearing my dog tags he most certainly would have found them and my game would have been up. At best I would have become a Prisoner of War or at least that's what they said at Geneva.

I walked on toward Fontenay and now was seeing quite a few Germans around on the roads and in the fields, all in camouflage type helmets. I noticed a lack of vehicles and self propelled guns and realized this must be part of a rear guard action and that surely I couldn't be far from my objective. I walked on into the village, which seemed strangely quiet.

Some damage was evident but appeared to be from small arms, and field artillery shells, instead of bomb damage like I had seen in other towns. In the town square some German soldiers were milling around working on various pieces of equipment, others, cat napping. I saw two soldiers trying to get an American Jeep started but I didn't have my rotor in my pocket at this time, so couldn't help. A few Frenchmen were also milling around but the Germans didn't pay them or me any attention. I did not hesitate but kept walking on north through the outskirts and out again into open country.

I walked on a mile or so and came to a point where the trees stopped and the road ran off through a clearing. As I was just about to step out into the clearing I heard voices over to my left and saw some Germans entrenched in the tall grass right at the edge of the clearing. I could tell they were yelling at me and motioning for me to get down. I promptly fell to the ground and one of the soldiers crawled over my way and motioned for me to follow him back into the grass. We crawled a few yards and came up to a group of them lying around in holes. Several near me started asking questions in German which, of course, I didn't understand. I couldn't pull my deaf act with the shells going overhead and hitting the ground every now and then nearby.

One of the soldiers asked me in English if I spoke English and I put on one of my dumbest don't understand a word you're saying faces. Thank God no one spoke French to me. We laid there for a while until one of the soldiers near me was hit in the leg and stomach with shrapnel. I readily caught on they wanted me to put the wounded soldier in a wheelbarrow, which was out in the ditch by the road, and wheel him back to a first aid station that luckily I had seen back on the road just after leaving Fontenay.

I dragged him through the grass, put him in the wheelbarrow and started wheeling. The wheeling was easy at first but it soon proved to be a real labor. The wounded kid didn't seem to be over seventeen years old and he was in great pain and had me stop frequently. I felt sorry for him in a way and looked to see if he had any medications on him to ease the pain, or cyanide to completely get rid of it.

I struggled on with the wheelbarrow and was finally able to deposit the boy in front of the first aid station which I supposed to be something like what we would call a field hospital. Some medical men came out and took him in and I turned to walk back into the village. Someone from the door yelled, like we would say "Hey". I froze in my tracks, afraid to play deaf and keep walking, turned around and saw a medic motioning to me to come back. When I got up to him he gave me the surprise of my life, two cigarettes and some kind of candy bar. I thanked him in my best French and bowed out and took off walking toward the village square as I certainly didn't want to retrace my steps back to the clearing.

I was now somewhat at a loss as to what to do. That feeling of so near and yet so far. I was off my beaten memorized tract, but knew that Bayeux could not be very far. So when I reached the square I turned west and walked on out of town without incident. Not too far out I saw two boys, young teenagers, standing by a gate leading up to a farm house. Because of the horse and plow there I figured they had been working in the field and were now just resting and talking. They eyed me as I was coming up the road and I was eyeing them back.

As I came along side they gave me a friendly greeting "Bon jour Messieur". I took a chance and said 'Allemands?' They pointed northwest. Naturally my accent put very curious looks on their faces.

I then told them that I was an American aviateur, and they momentarily gasped but came on with broad grins. I tried to put over what I was trying to do, and they caught on. One got a stick and scraped on the dirt where we were, just outside Fontenay. A line to the west a few miles was Tilly and just before I got there was

Captain E. J. Steiner welcoming me back to Kingscliffe.

a small dirt road headed north and the British were entrenched less than a mile up the road.

I gave them a few francs and started off following their directions, now wishing I had a few more slugs of Calvados.

I noticed the country was beginning to open up, not as many trees, more open fields, I could see farther in the distance. I also saw several large gun emplacements but very few soldiers around. Some Spitfires came over low, probably looking for targets to strafe and I saw the Germans hit one and he went off smoking to the north.

At the intersection of the road where I was to turn were knocked out British vehicles, a few tanks and trucks. Some had been knocked out by guns and a few up my road appeared to have been wrecked by mines.

I turned to the north and started down the small open road, watching carefully for mines. I have often thought how funny it must have looked to see a poor dumb French farmer out on this road jumping over places and side stepping other places, but I had to be careful where I placed each foot.

About a quarter of a mile farther I approached an intersection of hedgerows. I heard several Limey voices - "What the bloody hell is a French civilian doing out there?"

I then saw the good old British helmets.

I Had Made It; VIVA LA FRANCE!

As I hit the intersection one of the Limeys yelled at me in French. I yelled back, "Sorry, Tommy, I don't speak French". He looked surprised, took a tighter hold of his gun and said, "Don't pull that stuff around here," and motioned me with his gun to get over there. I hurriedly explained that I was an American pilot who had been shot down and had been working my way out of enemy territory. His look of 'Oh Yeah' showed that he didn't believe me one bit. I asked him to call his sergeant, or whoever was in charge, as I wanted to be taken back to the headquarters of this outfit.

A sergeant did appear, was given a brief explanation, kept his gun on me and we walked several hundred yards back to a tank. He ordered several soldiers to strip search me while he climbed in top to use the radio.

It was a cold day in Normandy to be standing there without a stitch on. One of the soldiers threw me a great coat and another handed me a mess kit cup of hot tea. I almost thought it was delicious but started to sweat at the thought that I might also be in for a procto search. But no, the sergeant got out of the tank, got briefed on my search while I put back on my clothes and we got in a jeep and drove several miles to a large headquarters house.

I was taken into a large room where several serious looking British officers, one a colonel, and an American major liaison officer, were waiting to see and talk with me. They seemed quite upset that I didn't have any identification on me except my forged French identity card but agreed that the picture on it was me. Being an evadee seemed to present a new and difficult problem to them. The American major asked all kinds of questions attempting to establish me as an American. With each answer all the gentlemen present began to ease up, relax, and even start to smile. One clincher answer I gave described my life as a student at Texas A&M and the fact that we had won the Southwest Conference two years in a row, '38 and '39, playing in the Sugar Bowl Jan. 1, 1940. My memory was poor on the game because I had been too sick on Slo-Gin Fizzes.

He had already mentioned he was from Dallas, which jogged my memory when he asked, "What prominent building in a large Texas city has an animal on top of it". I had worked at the 1936 Texas Centennial Fair in Dallas and knew the tall Magnolia Oil Corp. building had a large flying red horse (Pegasus) atop it. When the major said, "My God! He's got to be an American, a fellow Texan and a fellow Aggie," the rest of the group burst out laughing and a bottle of scotch was produced, over which they shook my hand, slapped me on the back and repeatedly said "Good show, good show."

The major took me in charge and drove me in his jeep to a newly established airfield for P47's. Luck was with me again as I knew some of the pilots. After they tired themselves of laughing at my story and costume, they arranged a flight for me on a hospital type aircraft back to England.

We deposited the wounded at a base in England and the pilots were good enough to fly me back to King's Cliffe.

I was a mild sensation when I walked into our pilots operations office as Jacques Robert and later at the officers' club where I got pretty drunk that night.

Next step was to report to Military Intelligence Service in London, Headquarters European Theater of Operations from which evolved Escape and Evasion Report No. 759, dated 20 June 1944.

"I MADE IT!" Photo of me at Kingscliffe upon my return, still dressed in my French civilian clothes.

CHAPTER 7: "It Finally Happened to Me, Too..."

The interrogation was one to make the Spanish Inquisition look anemic. The colonel, who was short, fat, and brisk, could ask questions as fast as an adding machine can click. No detail was too small to be gone over with a microscope. We finished at last and I felt like a mildewed rag. The colonel said I had acted coolly and skillfully, but that I had not really used my head. In this regard, the colonel stated my indiscretions: (1) I had thrown away my dog tags; (2) I could have been shot by the Germans for not having any kind of identification; (3) I was very foolish not to have kept my G.I. shoes. (The colonel considered these shoes important for walking. So did I. Jean's slippers caused my feet to holler, scream and groan with pain.); (4) I did not go the accustomed route of airmen, i.e., across the Pyrenees into Spain.

The coloncl then pointed out the French underground would have helped me to the Spanish border, where other members of the underground would have carried on. (I wanted to tell the colonel of the airmen who had died on the torturous ordeal of crossing the Pyrenees. I may have chosen the easier way, but I rightly thought I had a chance to live according to my plan.) The colonel further said I had not been so clever after all; that if there hadn't been so much front-line confusion, more attention would have been paid to a young "French" civilian wandering down the roads.

I was told by His Nibs I would remain in London for an indefinite period. He said, as I already knew, anyone shot down in enemy territory was not usually permitted to fly again in that theatre of operations. He added, significantly, such airmen were sent home. (I caught my breath on this one. But I kept my mouth shut. Often you can foul everything up in the army by saying just one word.) I was dismissed and told to report at headquarters each day.

Normally most everyone who evaded capture as I did, or escaped prison and got back, would be sent home for duty in the states. However, I returned to flying active combat missions. I didn't learn until years later that German Intelligence had a dossier on me and practically every other American fighter pilot in Europe and had I been shot down a second time and captured, I would have immediately been shot as a spy.

I cannot now recall the circumstances of my returning to combat.

One story was told to me by Jim Bradshaw at our 1980 Orlando reunion. He said I did receive orders to go home, but didn't want to go, so I borrowed Gen. Anderson's P47, flew across the field scattering pieces of the orders out of the cockpit.

I do recall Gen. Anderson calling me in for using his P47 for an unauthorized flight and damaging the landing gear upon return. How did I know that Jug had bricks in its belly; it was one heavy bird. Brigadier General Edward W. Anderson was then Commanding Gen. 67th Fighter Wing, 8th USAAF. He was one good Joe and had earlier been C.O. 20th Pursuit Group.

I was later to cause him more severe trouble, but that's another story.

Busted

In late June of 1944, as Operations Offcer of the 79th Fighter Squadron, I was promoted to Major. At the time of my upgrade, I was

After a heavy night of drinking at the Officer's Club, I took a heavy dunking in a static pool while returning back to the barracks. War is hell!

acting Commanding Officers of the Squadron and a little later became permanent C.O.

Upon hearing the news, a group of pilots from the Squadron decided that we should celebrate my promotion at the Officer's Club - on me. It was suggested that we should go to Peterborough and make the rounds, so six of us piled into a jeep and did just that. We didn't bother to stop at the front gate, we just waved and hollered at the guards. We made some rounds and started back to the base—still daylight.

A couple of MPs in a jeep started to chase us. I tried, but could not outrun their "hot rod" jeep. Words flew back and forth. I just about had the M.P. calmed down when suddenly one of the guys, a pugilistic type, "K/O'ed" one of the M.P.s—knocked him flat!!!! Guns were drawn—hands were raised—reinforcements were called in—and the next thing we heard was the CLINK of the jailhouse door!!!

It took a few days for the M.P.'s report to start working through channels. I knew I was in for it. I was charged with the following:
1. Unauthorized trip
2. No trip pass
3. Resisting arrest
4. Speeding
5. Overloaded Jeep
6. Assault on a Military Policeman
7. Urinating on the Street (not me)
8. Rioting in the Jailhouse (...all we did was make a little noise)

To say that Col. Cy Wilson, my Group C.O., was livid is way too mild—I thought that he was going to have a stroke. Upon receiving the first communication about the incident, you could hear his screaming voice all over the base. He made immediate preparations for us to drive to London. I was going to Eighth Air Force Headquarters to see General James Doolittle.

Whatever General Doolittle was doing, he stopped to receive the red-faced Cy Wilson and myself. I was expecting the worse. As

Cy was loudly talking, General Doolittle repeated my name a couple of times, and gave me a rather quizzical look. I immediately guessed what he was thinking—the international incident in Portugal in November of 1942—I was right!!!

I was asked to leave the room until called again. After sweating it out for what seemed like hours, actually 20 minutes. I was called back into the office. Col. Wilson had calmed down and was back to his original color. He sneered at me and said,

"Come to attention 2nd Lieutenant", rather sarcastically, "and wipe that smile off your face..."

In addition to being busted we were all grounded temporarily, and given fines, mine being the largest. Most of the fellows were Flight Commanders and the other squadrons had to furnish some flight C.O.s to keep the 79th in the air, for a short time.

After my promotional climb back up I'd had enough promotions to have become a Brigadier General. Col. Wilson promptly gave me the name General &*)%$@,!!!

There is no doubt about it, Col. Cy and General Doolittle were two of the finest people I have ever met. They knew that I wasn't "regular army."

Angers, Maine-et-Loire, France, August 1983
After only 39 years I returned to Europe for the first time since leaving the E.T.O. for the Zone of Interior in late '44.

The big event was to attend our 20th Ftr. Gp. dedication of our memorial monument in King's Cliffe. But very high on my list was to return to the place where I was shot down on 13 June '44 and visit with the French people, who at great risk to themselves, took me in and helped me start my evasion which, you have just read, turned out successfully.

For well over 30 years I had lost complete contact with them. I am greatly indebted to a fellow American, my friend, Anthony Piel, who works for the World Health Organization in Geneva, whose perseverance tracked down my long lost French helpers. I learned for the first time that Jean was now a professor in a college at Angers, long time married, with two grown children, and had named his son Jack, after me. Jack lives and works in Paris. He visited me in early '83 while in the U.S. on a business trip. A fine, personable

"My Sentimental Journey" - August 1983. Taken at the farmhouse where my P-38 crashed. The three children still lived there.

The armor plate headrest taken from behind the seat of my P-38. The family had taken it from the wreckage of my P-38 and had used it in their fireplace.

young man who speaks fluent English. He had gone to school in Pennsylvania and had tried to find me at that time.

I was most pleased that he was able to meet me at Charles De Gaulle Airport in Paris, after which we made a several hour drive down to Angers to visit his parents. During the last several hours many memories from 39 years ago came flooding back, so it was with mixed emotions that I walked in to their apartment and received the traditional French embrace from Jean. The full impact hit as to just what he had done for me back as a 17 year old kid in June '44. Without his help I could very well not be standing there that day. He had forgotten most of his English and I had long ago forgotten what little French I knew. We were both grateful for son Jack being a most able interpreter.

The best of wines were brought out and toast after toast given. They were all most delightful people.

My good friend Levon Agha-Zarian came up from Nice to join our group. He is one of the most colorful, enjoyable characters I've ever met – a Britisher by birth of American-French parents. He flew Spitfires and Hurricanes in the Battle of Britain as an RAF pilot. Then transferred to the Burma China India where he flew P47's (Jugs) with the RAF, 146th Assam Sq. Agha was the guiding spirit in organizing the P47 Thunderbolt Pilots Assoc. and served as its president during its first two years. Among his most noteworthy duties was when he was a personal aide to Lord Louis Mountbatten. I bring all this to your attention because I was honored that this most fabulous person would attend this little reunion. But that's the nature of good friends.

Christiane, Jean's wife and Jack's mother, and their daughter Carole prepared and served a most delicious meal. I never saw so many dishes used for one meal.

Jean had prepared a several day itinerary for us. The next day was a trip through the Loire (river) Valley, vineyards, wineries, chateau's (castles), a real good view of most beautiful countryside. The next day a tour of the area that I pretty much upset that 13 June '44.

CHAPTER 7: "It Finally Happened to Me, Too..."

Reception in Angers, August 1983. (Left to right) Levon Agha - Zarians, Leslie Atkinson, and me shaking hands with the Mayor of Angers.

French Television Interview - 1983. (Left to right) Jean Vileau, Jack Ilfrey, Odette Charuau.

The farm house and yard that I landed in by parachute, site of my P38 crash. It wasn't until now that I was learning the names of the places and the people involved. A trip to the bridge that we knocked out that day. This was all very nostalgic for me. We drank, talked and reminisced until the early morning. Jean still had the watch and gloves I was wearing that day I was shot down. Also the fountain pen and water proof maps I was carrying. I took back the few French francs I still had from the ones they had given me 39 years ago.

Next day we made a wonderful trip through the Loire River Valley chateaus. Beautiful weather was with us. Next day we paid a visit to the LaPossiniere railway bridge and to the LaMouliere farm where I had jumped in my parachute. The three children that I had remembered were still living there and the one I had called old man with the pitchfork was now really old and in a nursing home nearby. They had vivid memories of seeing my burning P38 streaking by, of me jumping out, landing on their farm house roof and bouncing down into the yard.

One brother remembered my asking for directions and that he had written in the sand, Caen 300 KM with an arrow pointing that way. They recalled my friends in the other P38s circling around and the noise they made. They said the Germans were in the area very soon after I ran off.

We visited the site of the crashed P38 about 300 meters away near another farm house. A man came up and told Jack, our interpreter, that he was a 13 year old boy on a tractor when the P38 roared 50' over him and crashed with all the pieces going away from him; otherwise he might have been killed. Another man had been on the train I strafed in the station at leLion-d-Angers, and recalled the sounds of my guns and explosion of the train's engine boilers. Before the Germans came to pick up the pieces of the P38 the French managed to get a couple of the propeller blades which they later honed into plow points.

They still had in the barn a gear box and ballast bag, and the armor plate that had been behind my body had been in the fireplace in the house radiating heat all these years.

From here we went a short distance to the small town of Gene' where at the town hall I was given a welcome ceremony by the present mayor and the mayor who was there in June '44.

We then went to Andigne where I stayed in '44 for another town hall reception.

Next day another much larger reception was held in the City Hall of Angers. Odette, the girl who had given me the bicycle, came from Nantes. Also my good friend Leslie Atkinson came from Paris for these ceremonies. Leslie is the European representative of the Air Force Escape and Evasion Society of which I am a member and I was honored that he would attend.

During the war there was a large underground organization in Europe that aided and helped many allied airmen escape and evade, just as Jean and his family and friends had helped me, however, they were not members of this organization.

Leslie, a Frenchman, had been a member of this organization and the French Resistance, and had aided many downed Allied airmen. After D-Day he became a scout and interpreter for the Americans. For the past many years he has been instrumental in getting American escape and evadees back together again with their wartime helpers.

An interview with all us was on French TV. All of the French I met during these past few days showed genuine friendly sincere feeling towards me and had nothing but praise for the Americans who helped liberate their country.

The last day with these wonderful hosts was a trip to the Brittany Atlantic coast where Jean and his wife had a cabin. Highlight of the trip for me was a stop in St. Nazaire and a tour through the German submarine pens, still standing majestically in their concrete and steel forms. I had made several missions escorting bombers to the pens and dive-bombing them. The allies tried and tried but were never very successful in knocking them out. The resort town of LaBaule was beautiful and I saw my first topless beach.

8

AND NOW THE BUZZ BOMBS

The buzz bomb season settled down late that afternoon. I was on the street, walking around aimlessly, when I heard a loud putter like a motorcycle. Suddenly the putter coughed and died. I had heard all about the V-1 buzz bombs from the pilot who had brought me over from France and I knew this buzz bomb was going to hit somewhere pretty close. You could sense that.

People stopped walking and stood rooted in their tracks. There came a kind of boom, then an ear-splitting roar. I felt the sidewalk beneath me move. Two blocks away I saw a building, lighted by fire, crumple into the street, and it seemed to me that tons of glass were crashing everywhere. There was something more terrifying about the robot pilot in a V-1 than there was when bombers came over with live pilots in them. There was an awful uncertainty...

An Englishman, who was standing near me, said it was a good thing D day came when it did or the Germans might have wiped London off the map with their buzz bombs. He said when the buzz bombs first started coming over, all the anti-aircraft guns in London would open upon them but after a week of this, the military decided not to shoot at them and maybe some of the bombs would go on past London, which they did. I was astonished at the casual way the Britisher talked. From his tone of voice, we might have been in the Savoy-Plaza Bar, having a Scotch-and-soda, and I wondered if we Americans would have stood up as well if the tables had been turned.

By this time the fire fighters, rescue squads, and the Home Guard were on the scene, and they all swept into action. I tried to do what I could to help but the English moved too swiftly for me. I walked back to my room at the hotel but not to sleep.

It didn't take London long to set up a good defense against the robot enemy. On later missions I saw great masses of balloons several thousand feet high in the air. These balloon barrages were centered southeast of London—between London and the Channel—and there was also a large concentration of guns placed in this area, which was known as "Flak Alley." This strategy greatly eliminated the number of bombs that got over London.

The people were taking to the air raid shelters, as they had done during the blitz. In the early part of the afternoon the Londoners would begin making their makeshift beds in the shelters and in the corridors and stations of the subways. By 11:00 P.M. one could hardly get on and off the subways for all the sleepers around.

We Americans tried to be pretty fatalistic about the buzz bombs. We wouldn't go to the air raid shelters. We figured sort of foolishly if our time had come, the bomb with our number on it would find us wherever we were—in the American Melody Bar or in the air raid shelter.

The night before I left London I had gone to bed early. I had spent hours at headquarters that day waiting to see the colonel, only to be told nothing save to come back the following day. I was mortally knocking it off when the next thing I knew I was sitting squarely on my behind on the floor and the most awful rocking you've ever felt. For my money, the hotel was doing a Betty Grable rhumba, and I clipped it down to the air raid shelter and spent the rest of the night there—to hell, with that stuff about your number being on it....

The buzz bombs seemed to pursue me. Next morning on my way to headquarters I could tell we were going to have an unwelcome visitor. The people on the street were freezing up and waiting to see if they were going to have to fall flat on the sidewalk. Sure enough we had to fall flat, and it would have to be raining that morning.

The English showed a courageousness during the buzz bomb season that was unequaled by anyone else so far as my personal knowledge went. They'd go to work in the morning, not knowing if they'd have an office to work in, and in the evening when they started home they'd never know whether they had a wife or a home to come back to.

The uncertainty was far worse than when the bombers came over. The Britishers had warning then, but the buzz bomb was right there—bringing sudden slaughter, ravaged homes and buildings, and anguish and sorrow.

CHAPTER 8: And Now the Buzz Bombs

My crew and I standing in front of my P-51D5-NA-#44-13761 MC-I. This shot was taken in September of 1944 when I was Commanding Officer of the 79th Fighter Squadron.

9

BACK TO DUTY

For a change, the colonel sent for me at once when I arrived at headquarters, but he was slightly annoyed because I was late, buzz bombs notwithstanding. He said he had good news for me, and as I hadn't even hoped to be able to go home, I said to myself, "Yes, I bet you have." First, the colonel informed me, I was to make a tour of the fighter bases in England and tell the French story. He said my experience would be helpful to the boys and I could give them hints that might aid them to escape should any of the pilots be forced down in France.

The thought of the "lecture" tour griped the hell out of me, but after my first appearance at Ipswich, I started getting a kick out of it. I felt silly talking to the boys at first but was able to answer many of their questions. The whole thing was just a matter of reliving the French episode over again, and I really enjoyed traveling around on this "lecture" tour. I was meeting lots of new people and seeing some of my old friends, and many of the boys I had trained at Santa Ana.

When I got back to base the changeover from P-38s to P-51s had not been entirely completed and I had a lot of work to do. All the P-38s and P-47s in the Eighth Air Force were being transferred to the Ninth and were being used for tactical purposes in support of the ground troops on the Continent. All fighter groups in the Eighth Air Force were being equipped with new P-51s, and the Mustang was proving to be a better all-around airplane than the P-38 for long range escort in our strategic work. Our morale went up, our victories went up, and our losses went down. Added to the superior qualities of the P-51 were the "G" suit, or anti-blackout suit, and the new British gyroscopic gun sight. These things gave us a better feeling of aggressiveness because whereas we were limited in the P-38s in diving characteristics and maneuvering, the P-51 could do more things. Now we had more fighting spirit. I had no more fear of flying around Berlin than I used to around Los Angeles, with several of my buddies, of course; but we were all probably wishing it was Los Angeles.

The anti-blackout suit kept the pilots from blacking out when exceptional gravitational pull was encountered, such as pulling out of a dive or short and quick turns. A human body can only stand from three to four Gs, that is, three or four times the weight of your

Ted Slanker - 77th Fighter Squadron pilot standing in front of his P-51D "The Butcher Boy." The name of his aircraft came when Slanker buzzed a herd of cattle, causing them to stampede. When the incident was over, it was found that several of the cattle were dead. The name stuck.

Major Glenn Miller and his Orchestra made a visit to Kingscliffe on October 3, 1944. Miller met a face from the past that day, Sergeant Raymond C. Fray who dated Miller's sister Irene in high school.

CHAPTER 9: Back to Duty

Glenn Miller at Kingscliffe October 3, 1944.

Left to Right: Bill Lewis, 79th FS pilot, Sgt. Rob Robinson, T/Sgt. Ethan Schrader, Crew Chief Sgt. Tony Kublin.

body pulling against you before blacking out, which occurs when all the blood drains from the head causing temporary blindness.

The "G" suit was a zipped-on suit, which had a large rubber bladder around the abdomen and also bladders around the calves and thighs of the legs. A hose was attached to the suit which connected to the vacuum system of the ship and any abnormal gravitational pull would cause the bladders to inflate with increasing pressure against the abdomen and legs, forcing the blood to stay in the head.

With this invention, the pilot could withstand as many Gs as the airplane could, and in the case of a P-51 this was up to nine or ten Gs; more than that and the wings would have probably been pulled off. We wouldn't be caught without our G suit on.

Ground crews of the 55th Fighter Squadron at Kingscliffe. (Credit - Ken Sumney)

Pilots synchronizing their watches after mission briefing. Group C.O. Cy Wilson shown in the middle of the photo with Mae West on.

Jack Ilfrey in the cockpit of P-51D. Note the field installed Spitfire rear-view mirror.

We nicknamed our new gyroscopic sight, the K14, the "No-Miss-'Em" gun sight. It took care of all deflection and skid and when it was properly lined up, you just pulled the trigger and got yourself a German airplane...or so it says here.

Cy Wilson was now our new group commander. I had known Cy back in the States and he was very eager to go overseas. So when an order came to ship out five second lieutenants, he put down the names of four lieutenants and himself on the order. He drew a "dud"—Iceland—and after almost a year there he came to England and took over our group. Cy helped me a lot with the duties of squadron commander. He was a well-liked CO and he'd never ask anyone to do anything he wouldn't do. When it came to flying and leading missions, Cy was tops. He had to be the first to shoot at anything, and he was a great help to our morale.

I soon found out being squadron commander involved much more responsibility than I had anticipated. I had always felt when I had troubles, I had no one to blame but myself. Now I had 250 men who could get me into trouble and get me into trouble they did—twenty-four hours a day. I was also responsible for all of the squadron's equipment, and it seemed funny to write off lost airplanes and other material running into hundreds of thousands of dollars. I was lucky in having a good "exec." a ground officer, and a good first sergeant. I was luckier still in having an outfit with good spirit and a high morale. We were bothered very little with the so-called officer caste system. After all, the pilots were the ones in the fighter squadron who went out and got shot at and the enlisted men respected them for that, if nothing else. The ground crews took great pride in their ships and the pilots. Each airplane had one pilot assigned to it and a ground crew consisting of a crew chief (technical sergeant), and assistant crew chief, a radio maintenance man, and an armorer who took care of the guns and gun camera.

The airplanes were divided into four flights for maintenance and we had a weekly contest among our flights. The one who had the most airplanes in commission and the greatest number of com-

55th Fighter Squadron Hanger and Engineering Shack at Kingscliffe.

77th Fighter Squadron Pilots: Left to Right: Hamberton, Geiger, Van Woert, Alison, Einhaus, Garner, Purse. (Credit - Ken Sumney)

CHAPTER 9: Back to Duty

Captain Earl Hower, 55th FS, 20th FG standing in front of his P-51D #44-13759, "Flying Dutchman."

Ernest Fiebelkorn, top 20th Fighter Group ace, 11 victories.

bat hours flown for the week were usually given a beer "bust" by the pilots who flew the planes in the winning flight.

Usually at the end of each month the pilots would give a beer "bust" for the men in the squadron, and we tried to have these beer "busts" on nights when we knew there would be no flying next day and the men wouldn't have to get up early and get the ships ready for flight. Shortly after supper all of us would gather in the group briefing room and go over everything that had taken place during the month. Larkin, our intelligence officer, would describe the nature of all the missions the pilots had flown. Combat films from the gun cameras would be shown with explanations from the pilots. If one of the flyers had had an interesting encounter with the Jerries, he would tell about it. On one occasion I even told the French story! After all questions were answered, we would gather in the hangar for the "blowing of the suds." There would be lots of singing, jokes cracked, and a few individual pantomimes, and we'd introduce the new pilots. The officers and men would all let their hair down and I'll never forget when I was introduced as the new squadron com-

77th Fighter Squadron in formation over England.

THE BRASS: Left to Right: Col. Harold Rau, C.O. 20th Fighter Group; Col. Ben Kelsey - USAAC Chief Test Pilot; Lt. Col. Robert Montgomery, Deputy Group C.O.; and Lt. Col. Russell Gustke, C.O. 77th Fighter Squadron.

Control Tower at Kingscliffe. Fall - 1944.

mander. It seems the boys had a custom before the night was over of giving the new C.O. a very informal initiation by stripping off his clothes and giving him a good rubdown with beer.

Maybe we were lenient in the Air Corps but whatever our attitude was I think it helped to bring about a better means to an end. Whenever I heard any griping about food and living conditions I always reminded the men they were better off than most of the other boys scattered all over the world. They had places to go and things to do. It wasn't like home, of course, but it wasn't Africa, or sleeping in tents in Italy, or fighting in the South Pacific. We all had a hell of a lot to be grateful for in England.

The fighter squadron's morale was always higher than in the bomber squadrons. We did not have death brought so close to home as the bombers did. When a fighter was lost or shot down, he just failed to come home. He was missing to the men. But many times crippled bombers came back to base with one or more dead on board, and the men at base got a firsthand view of death. Their buddies were not just missing with hopes of still being alive. They were right there—dead.

Cy Wilson was a great one for ground strafing. He literally ate it up. All of us boys used to love to follow him. He had such a good knack for finding locomotives and other excellent targets to strafe. Cy always flew with a big cigar in his mouth, a la Churchill, and I think the only time he ever took it out of his mouth was when he was flying at high altitudes and had to wear his oxygen mask.

The last time I saw Cy he had a cigar in his mouth, but I'm sure he wasn't smoking it. He had just bailed out into the North Sea, off the Danish coast, and was sitting in his dinghy, shaking his fist at

79th Fighter Squadron - fall of 1944. Jack Ilfrey, Squadron C.O. standing left of the prop.

CHAPTER 9: Back to Duty

George Merriman, pilot and groundcrew; 79th Fighter Squadron.

79th Fighter Squadron pilots; (left to right) Bradshaw, Baldwin, Heiden.

Flight Line, Kingscliffe; 55th Fighter Squadron Ordinance Section.

"An army runs on its stomach." Mess Hall Cooks, Kingscliffe 1943-1945.

BELOW: 77th Fighter Squadron / 20th Fighter Group in early 1945.

77th Fighter Squadron in formation over in East Anglian countryside.

us. We had been strafing an airdrome on the West Danish coast, and Cy had been hit. He managed to fly out to sea several miles before ditching his ship.

We tried to get Air Sea Rescue to pick him up but we were almost 400 miles from the English coast, which was out of the operating limit of Air Sea Rescue. We hated to leave Cy there in his dinghy, but later we heard he was a prisoner of the Germans and still later, after V-E Day, he came back to the group.

Arch Whitehouse (left) - British WW I ace and WWII war correspondent and 20th FG C.O. Cy Wilson - September 1944.

My going away party. Kingscliffe Officer's Club.

10

TWO RIDE IN A MUSTANG

It was the 20th of November, 1944. On this particular afternoon I led a flight of P51Ds, of the 79th Fighter Squadron, to rendezvous and escort a pair of P-38 "Photo Joes" on a mission to Berlin. These were modified P-38s, called F-5s. Instead of carrying the normal compliment of machine guns in the nose of the fuselage, they were modified to carry reconnaissance cameras.

As we flew towards Berlin we encountered light bursts of flak along our route. The Flight then turned to the south and headed towards Magneburg, and then towards the Bonn area. The F-5s were photographing an area where our bombers had attacked an airfield and a synthetic oil plant earlier that day. The F-5s radioed home that they were now low on film and fuel and were now steering a course for England.

After an escort was completed, it was a common ritual to hit the deck and search for ground targets on our way back home to England. We spiraled down through a hole and sure enough for plenty of "targets of opportunity." There were columns of trucks, tanks, and other equipment heading west towards the front lines.

I organized the formation for a strafing attack, and we headed towards the deck. Our Flight made several passes over the columns, and we managed to destroy many vehicles in the process. We had expended a lot of ammunition, and our fuel supply was getting critical. It was shortly after 1600 hours, so I decided to set a course for England.

We were in a good tight formation as we headed west towards Kingscliffe. We flew as low as possible to stay away from a nasty weather front that was beginning to form to our west. We screamed across the countryside just over the tree-tops. While over Maastricht, Holland, we picked up some heavy ground fire. We veered right and headed toward the North, away from the city and all the "ack-ack." At that time, my wingman 1st Lt. Duane Kelso radioed that his aircraft was hit and losing power rapidly.

We climbed to about 700 to 800 feet and now were in poor visibility. I radioed back to Kelso that I had sighted an abandoned airstrip a few miles back that appeared to be an emergency type strip surrounded by trees and a few bombed-out aircraft scattered around it.

I pointed it out and told him to try for it while I attempted to cover him. Knowing we were almost out of fuel, I told the other three boys that they were on there own.

I told Kelso that the strip doesn't look bad, use your own judgment whether to attempt a wheels down landing. He in turn gave me a thumbs up signal and dropped his gear down.

We circled around still picking up heavy gunfire, as Kelso set-up to make his approach. He made a rather hairy wheels down landing, stopping right near the edge of the trees. He climbed out of the cockpit and dashed away from the plane. I looked down at him as I flew over the end of the strip. There he was with a big grin on his face, thumbs up and all.

Kelso was a good pilot, and an excellent wingman. He followed me anywhere and I couldn't help feeling very close to him at that particular moment. Without giving it another thought, I instinctively circled around the field to set-up an approach for landing. I thought of several instances that my comrades had saved my life, and I theirs. Friendships forged in combat are never forgotten.

I threw down my wheels and flaps and went in for another hairy landing. Kelso had the presence of mind to get away from his aircraft, because the Germans were still trying to hit it. He ran about a hundred yards or so to the end of the strip figuring I would turn around and take off from the way I came in. God what a scary landing. The field was full of mud and holes, but the "Go Buggy" made it.

I taxied a short distance up to Kelso, set the brakes, and jumped out onto the wing. I threw my parachute and dinghy off and motioned Kelso to climb into the cockpit. He sat down into the bucket seat and I climbed in on top of him. We soon discovered that four legs impaired my ability to operate the rudder controls, so I stood up and he crossed his legs and I sat down on them. We had no time for seat or harness adjustments. I almost scalped myself trying to close the canopy. Thank God it was a P-51 "D" model.

Kelso was pretty shaken by the whole incident. I thought that I would make light of our circumstance and ease him down a little, so I turned to him and screamed, "for Christ's sake Kelso, don't get a "hard-on" and send me through the canopy!!!!" With my head and neck bent down and my knees almost to my chin, I shoved the throttles forward and raced across the potholed field. I almost castrated myself pulling the stick back into my crotch, but we managed to clear the trees.

Renewing Old Acquaintances

In the early fall I went to London to appear on Ben Lyons's radio program, "The Combat Classroom of the Air," which was broadcast to the States. It was fun giving our opinions and answering questions, and I was delighted to meet Ben Lyons, who was clean-cut looking and most likable. He was then a lieutenant colonel in the Public Relations Department of the Eighth Air Force and was doing a swell job. I remembered Ben when he had been a star in the silent movies and my only disappointment was in not meeting his wife, Bebe Daniels, who was away in Italy on a USO tour. After the broadcast, Ben invited the ten of us who had appeared on the program out to his house, just outside of London, for a big feed and party.

The next day I 'phoned up my old girl friend, Peggy Thurlow, whom I had met when I was in London in '42. It was quite an act to work the British telephone. Most of the telephone booths were on the outside, on the corners and near entrances to buildings. The booths were situated somewhat like our fire boxes except the booths were completely enclosed and operating the telephone was more or less a process. The local calls cost a tuppence, two coppers, and a copper was about as big as our 50-cent piece. When you lifted the receiver, the operator said, "Where are you calling?" You gave her the number and place you were calling and dropped the right amount of money in the penny slot, the sixpence slot, or the shilling slot, depending upon where you were calling. Then you waited and if your party answered, you had to push button "A" before you could talk, and if your party didn't answer, you pushed button "B" and your money was returned to you. Fortunately, Peggy was still in London, on her government job, and I rode one of the double-deck busses out to Shepherd's Bush. After we had tea, Peggy asked me to accompany her to the Limehouse District, where she had to attend to some business. I had never seen the famous Limehouse District, and after I had seen it, it was not hard to imagine how various writers had produced such compelling pictures of dirt, squalor, and foul-smelling people. There was nothing interesting about Limehouse to me. All I saw was filth and degeneracy at its lowest. Civilization seemed to have by-passed the district. Peggy said she knew of a nice little restaurant in Soho where we could have dinner. The restaurant was nice enough but the food was terrible. Even the bread was greasy. But Soho itself was colorful with its French, Swedish, Italian, and other foreign clubs and restaurants. Soho, like the rest of London, was not particularly clean, but it was shining in comparison with the Limehouse District.

While we were eating, Peggy told me she had met a lot of nice Americans and a good many of not-so-nice Americans. She said the not-so-nice Americans seemed to think every English girl they met was just another Piccadilly "Commando," and she wondered if this was their attitude at home. I assured her it wasn't. I sort of apologized for the Americans who left their manners at home the minute they stepped off U.S. soil. Peggy told me she had been going with a lieutenant in the O.S.S. Headquarters and how amazed she had been when he brought out a Sunday edition of the Los Angeles Times with fifty-four pages in it. The English newspapers never had more than four or six pages and not a line of advertising during the war. Peggy couldn't understand why our newspaper had so much advertising when newsprint was severely rationed in England. She commented on the fact there was so little news from Washington in the Times, and I explained we Americans rarely ever saw a Washington paper and that news in the U.S. was not slanted from the angle of our nation's capital. I reminded Peggy the leading newspapers were all published in London and were sent out to every town in the British Isles in a matter of a few hours, and were more or less national newspapers, while our Washington, D.C., papers were just local.

Peggy said although the Britishers did put up with a lot from the Americans, most of them understood that men in the Air Corps and combat men from the Continent were entitled to three or four days of wine, women and song in London, and that the English did not begrudge them their sprees. And then she smiled and said, "One of our favorite expressions about the Americans is that they are overpaid, overdressed, oversexed, and over here."

Missions were becoming fairly routine now. Only once in a great while did we meet any German opposition, and the only time we'd lose anybody would be on ground strafing missions when they'd get hit by flak or lost in bad weather, which we were experiencing over the Continent. And speaking of bad weather, storms in the air are not as we see them on the ground. Most of the storms on the ground are large or small thunderheads which sometimes go up

Lt. Duane Kelso

CHAPTER 10: Two Ride in a Mustang

as high as 8,000 to 10,000 feet, and thunderheads are easily avoided by flying around or over them, and in most cases are avoided because of the vicious up-and-down currents in them. The higher an airplane goes the smoother the air gets and the faster it gets. It's not uncommon at 30,000 feet to encounter 150 to 200 m.p.h. winds, but it is unusual to encounter any clouds, as the ordinary ones do not go quite that high.

One of the most dangerous things you encounter in flying is when moisture from the clouds forms ice on the wings. This, however, can usually be avoided by going down to warmer levels or up out of the ice range.

We were beginning to see the V-2 rockets fired from Germany and shooting many miles above us, heading for London. We were also seeing a few German jets and occasionally some of our boys would box a jet in and when he came down they'd nail him. We were no match for the jet except that it didn't have any range and when out of gas, it had to come down and couldn't dive any faster than we could.

Urinating Over Europe
On long trips of four to five hours or even longer it often became necessary to relieve one's self. All fighter planes were equipped with a relief tube but being strapped down tight and at 30,000 feet, with all the heavy clothing on, oxygen mask, helmet, "G" suit, etc., it was quite a feat if one was able to successfully complete this maneuver without mishap. I'll never forget one mission when I was deep in Germany and it became quite necessary to relieve myself. About half way through, the tube, being stopped up, became full and I was left holding it, wondering what to do next. I decided to empty it on the floor by my feet, and then I repeated the process all over. I had just gotten through when someone yelled we were being jumped by the Jerries. In evading I applied some negative pressure to the controls, causing all the urine on the floor to shoot upwards where it scattered over my front windshield. When the warm urine hit the very cold glass at 30,000 feet, and where the temperature was at -50 degrees below zero, it froze over solid, blanking out my vision. I frantically tore off my gloves and scraped furiously at the ice with my fingers and made enough clear space on the glass so I could see out the front a little. And there I was at 30,000 feet with a fogged-up, urinated windshield. And what did I do. . .

11

RUSSIA

Frantic VI Shuttle Mission to Russia Sept. 1944

We had been told again and again our group would probably make a shuttle run to Russia, Italy and back. We had been alerted and prepared ourselves several times, but the trip never materialized. It had all started when Warsaw was being besieged and the Polish government in London was begging us to drop supplies. The American and British authorities were in favor of helping the Poles, but the ever-suspecting Russians said NO.

In September we finally did go on the shuttle run. Our group of sixty-five P-51 fighters escorted around seventy B-17s to a target near Chemnitz, southeastern Germany.

Shortly after target time we ran into bad weather and the fighters not only got separated from the bombers over the middle of Poland but also got separated from themselves.

My squadron became separated, too. I had a flight of four with me and we dived down below the cloud levels and broke out of the overcast at 2,000 feet, finding ourselves right over the Russo-German Front, which, from my maps, appeared to be on the Vistula River. We really had to study our maps to find out where we were, and we soon spotted the rather large city of Lublin. It was fairly easy then to set a course for Kiev. The country was flat through here and reminded me of Kansas and Missouri. After an hour or so we came to the Dnepr River and saw Kiev off to the right. We found our base at Pyriatin and most of the boys surprised us by finding their way into Pyriatin. We still had several men unaccounted for and learned later one of the boys had been shot down by ground fire near the Vistula and another had been forced down by Russian fighters.

The Russians had barely greeted us when they started swarming over our airplanes, examining them minutely, and, of course, we were proud to show every detail of our good machines. But presently we saw the Russians act just the opposite way. There was an old plane of World War I vintage on the field, and this plane was so well-guarded one couldn't get a good look at it. Even when one of our Douglas C-47s flew in with Russian pilots, a heavy guard was immediately thrown around the cargo ship. We said, "Hell, we don't care to inspect that plane. Most of us have flown it at sometime or other."

The Russians on this base were outwardly nice to us but it was only surface. They watched us like hawks.

There were no buildings on the field and we were housed in tents and ate our meals in a large tent some distance away. The food was strictly American, served by Russian girls. While the girls were large, they were well-built, and they could have used a good bath. They had no chance for glamour in their uniform and boots and no cosmetics. One normally brave pilot, Stud, said, "Too rugged for me!"

79th Squadron Pilots ready for Shuttle Mission to Russia. Note the US flag armband on our sleeves.

Piryatin, Ukraine. Myself (kneeling) and Glen Webb with Russian soldiers and civilians. September 12, 1944.

CHAPTER 11: Russia

Glen Webb and I with two Russian soldiers.

The Russian officers were under the impression these girls were to keep us company while we were at the base, but we were not used to having women fight and live with us, as the Russians were, and our commanders rejected the offer for us. I am sure, however, some of the boys were highly entertained.

Night life was extinct. Consequently, we spent our evening hours in the small club—another tent—trying to drink vodka with the Russians. They could keep the stuff as far as I was concerned. A couple of the officers spoke English and we had amazing conversations, what with our expressions and the Russians knowing only textbook English.

There was one woman officer who acted as an interpreter, and I think she understood a lot of our slang than she let on. After the vodka began to take its powerful effect, we'd say, "Hi, babe," and her face went blank, but her eyes showed she knew what we were saying. She was not exciting.

We were supposed to go on a few missions with the Russians attacking targets at the front, but nothing happened for a day or two and we didn't like the inactivity. So we asked permission to fly and test a few of our airplanes. This was refused. It seemed if you wanted to fly your plane you had to get Uncle Joe's permission, and the telephone system was not so good...We asked if we might go into Kiev. Again the answer was no, and it looked like we were not going to see anything of Russia.

Supposedly we were not allowed to go off the base, but combat fighter pilots were not to be deterred by a little order like that, so we tried to swipe, I mean borrow, a Studebaker (the Russian word for all trucks, which they were). Lend lease again. Unsuccessful in this we did manage a couple of 4 passenger jeeps, (lend-lease — why not?) So with 7 to 8 passengers each we made dusty tracks off the base. We had not as yet learned the Russian word for Halt or Stop. Don't know if we ever did. Seems like some of us did recognize the (lend lease) Springfields of the Spanish American war. There was not much to see in the town of Piryatin. Dirty, dusty streets, no cars running, no stores open, nothing to buy. All the populace we saw, kids and women were shabbily dressed and looked underfed. But then we must remember the Russian common people had been through hell at the hands of the Germans.

Curious kids gathered around us and all seemed very polite, offering us rubles for a few things we had on us, candy, gum, cigarettes. They did not beg as the children had done in all the N. African countries I had visited. We wouldn't take the children's money for the things we gave them, but we did take a ruble or two for souvenirs.

The bombers were stationed at Poltava, which was about eighty or ninety miles from Pyriatin, and one night during our stay, the Germans came over and bombed the field at Poltava, knocking out several of our bombers. The Russians got mad about the bombing, saying it was our fault for not having the proper anti-aircraft equipment. It never occurred to the Russians we would have had to bring such equipment from England, and we assumed they had anti-aircraft protection of their own. The Russians had no system at all for air raid warnings.

The days at Pyriatin were long and hot and the nights were cool. We slept in our sleeping bags on an American cot and wondered when this waiting would come to an end. While we knew this trip was along the good-will line, still we were supposed to have flown a few missions, hoping the Russians would eventually come through with bases in Siberia so we could operate against Japan. Nothing worked out, so we said good-bye to Russia, with no regrets. We had done nothing. We had seen nothing.

We took off, with the bombers, for a target near Budapest. It was an eventless trip across the Balkans, Rumania, Hungary, Yugoslavia, to the Adriatic. We noticed the towns in the Balkans were square, like in olden times. From the air, the cities seemed to stop abruptly and were built like fortresses.

I took my squadron to a base near Foggia on the spur of the Italian boot, and who should I find there but my old outfit, the 94th Fighter Squadron. Nearly all of the enlisted men were still with the group but I knew only a few of the ground officers. After leaving

We carried this chit ID card with us to Russia proclaiming us as USAAC pilots.

Curious fighter pilots "borrow" a jeep to see the Russian sights.

79th pilots with Russian children.

North Africa the men had been stationed in Sicily and Sardinia, and had been in Italy for sometime. They were living in tents, in the mud, and life was anything but easy. Roy Silvers, my old crew chief, was there, too, and we reminisced by the hour.

These boys had really had it rugged. Living in tents for almost two years, they didn't know what soap and water were like. Yes, we had it pretty nice in England...

It was warm in this part of Italy and for the first time we were able to wear our khaki clothes. It was always too cool in England to wear anything but O.D.s. The first thing we did was to commandeer a few vehicles and take off for the beach. It was wonderful, swimming in the Adriatic. The water was warm like the Gulf of Mexico, and the sun felt good after all those clammy months in England. We bought cantaloupes and watermelons from the Italian farmers and proceeded to have a party on the beach.

In an au naturel state the water felt good after all those clammy days in England. It didn't last long, however, as a couple of M.P.s came by. The day of the nude beaches was not in vogue and they made us get out.

That night the 94th Fighter Squadron gave us a party, with food, an orchestra, and brought in some Italian girls from Foggia. We liked the girls, and thought them a little more chic than the English girls. They had better figures and were nice dancers. Colonel Rau, who had led our group on this mission, made a trip over to Naples in a P-38 "Piggy-Back" and picked up his wife, who was a WAC working in headquarters there. He brought her to the base especially for our party and the party really got going when the men started dragging out their carefully hoarded liquor.

The next day in Foggia we were able to buy some souvenirs. There was a lot of mother-of-pearl in the Adriatic and the Italians had made it up into attractive bracelets, necklaces, and rings. They had also taken large pieces of shrapnel out of which they made ashtrays, statues, letter openers, and even bowls. There was a nice Red Cross Canteen in Foggia where you could hear a stringed band, with mandolins, violins, and guitars play while you munched on doughnuts and drank coffee.

The countryside was pretty, with its orchards and vineyards, but the little villages we passed through were dirty and the children were running around naked.

The bombers had gone back to England and we had one more day left in sunny Italy. I decided I'd ride over to Bari and see my friend, Alden Sherry, who was working in Air Force Headquarters there and whom I've mentioned as being one of the aces in the Hat-in-the-Ring Squadron in World War I—my old squadron on my first tour of duty in '42 and '43.

The "Madam" was the same as ever, full of good talk, reminiscing about the old days in the 94th Fighter Squadron, when he had fought with such pilots as Rickenbacker, Quentin Roosevelt, Frank Luke (the "balloon buster"), and James Norman Hall. I told him we of the 94th had not produced pilots equal to the caliber of these men. He didn't agree, saying we'd had it a little rougher than they did in the days of 1918, that they even had a sort of comradeship with the Germans. He meant by this the pilots saw and talked with captured Germans and even went over battles they'd fought against each other. He said sometimes they went so far as to wave to each other when they had run out of ammunition. This all seemed a little far-fetched to me. And he went on to say how we'd had bad living conditions in North Africa, and recalled when we first went to Africa every one of our missions was a bitter struggle, for the Luftwaffe had more planes than we did and the German crews were more battle-wise.

He told me a little of the First Fighter Group's history, how it was activated in early 1918 and was composed of many pilots who had already had experience with the Lafayette Escadrille and other French squadrons. The first commander of the group was Major Lufbery, the originator of several of the flying tactics that we now used. He said in those days the squadrons operated only within a radius of 150 miles, while we had started combat operations in early '42, with our first victory in Iceland, and traveled all the way from England to Africa, and back up to Italy. He said we had one big advantage, and that was the parachute, which had saved many fliers' lives. He told me after I left the organization in Africa, the First

CHAPTER 11: Russia

Left to Right: Glen Webb and Frank Roark swimming in the Adriatic Sea.

Getting out; left to right Glen Webb, Jess Yaryan, and "beefcake" Jesse Carpenter.

Fighter Group had had the honor of escorting the planes of President Roosevelt and Churchill to the Yalta Conference. This was something I did not know. Sherry reminded me I had a tradition behind me in two wars. He said that we had acquitted ourselves well, that we had a tradition to carry into the future... the future—that was something I'd soon be thinking about. My second tour of combat would be completed soon. I could start thinking about home...

Most of France had now been liberated, and we had nothing to do on the return trip except fly and we took it leisurely. We saw the pile of rubble that used to be Cassino. We circled over Rome and picked out Vatican City, the Coliseum, and then on out to the Isle of Capri, past Corsica, which appeared to be a very beautiful island from the air. We crossed the French Riviera coast and it was equally beautiful. We wanted to circle and have a look at the Riviera, but about this time we ran into a large weather front, and when we tried to climb over the front, my airplane started acting up in the high altitude, with the motor cutting out intermittently. I decided against risking the trip across the Channel and landed at the airdrome, Villacouble, just south of Paris.

All along the route of my bicycle trip through occupied France, I remember seeing signs such as Paris, 100 kilometers, Paris 50 kilometers, etc., and was tempted several times to go and see the great city I had heard so much about. Now, being so close to Paris, I couldn't pass up the chance.

Two P-47s from the Ninth Air Force landed shortly after I did, both with motor trouble. The pilots had the same idea I did about seeing Paree. The mechanics told us we'd have four or five hours of waiting, so we took off, hitchhiking.

From the minute I stepped out of the truck, beauty and color rushed out to greet me. Here was a beauty that enveloped you, creating a mood that was warm and intoxicating. The girls, riding their bicycles on the streets, waved to us. They had pretty legs and they didn't care who knew it. The mademoiselles were vivacious, like the American girls, and seemed to be endowed with a special capacity for dazzling smiles. We were practically overcome by the French men and women coming up, embracing us, offering to buy drinks. The fact that we had no French money didn't seem to make any difference. The normally thrifty Parisians were generous and treated us to everything. They couldn't do enough for the Americans, their great liberators. We were still an oddity and the American uniform was still looked upon with high esteem.

We did a quick tour of Montmartre and at one place we were served by topless waitresses.

We had to say good-bye to Paree after no more than a bowing acquaintance. It was an enchanting city and the French seemed to have a special gift for living and making you welcome.

12

EPILOGUE

In December 1944 I finished my second tour of combat having a combined total of 142 Combat Missions. 528 Combat Hours. Three fourths or more of these in the P-38 and the balance in the P-51.

I recieved orders back to the Zone of Interior and after a 30-day leave was assigned to McChord Field, Tacoma, Washington, as a Troop Commander. My Administrative duties consisted of helping in planning for the invasion of Japan and assisting the processing of returning troops, especially after V-J day.

I was formally discharged in late September 1945 and had three months terminal leave. During this time, I wrote the first version of this book. In late 1946 my good friend, John Landers, was flying a corporate aircraft for a firm in Ft. Worth. He recommended me for the same type of job with a company in Dallas. I went up to Beechcraft Co. in Wichita, Kansas, and purchased a brand new C-45 (military version) for $3500.00. I flew it to Spartan Aircraft in Tulsa, Oklahoma, and had it converted to a D-18 corporate aircraft.

My bosses, along with myself, were fun-loving people and we got along fine. However, being away for most of the time, helped to break up my family life.

In the early 1950s my 20-20 vision began to fade and glaucoma started to set in. My flying career was virtually over. I knew that I would now have to pursue another type of career. While visiting San Antonio, I saw an ad in the newspaper by a bank which said that they were looking for someone that had a military background. So I checked it out. I walked in, thinking that at least it would be a stop-gap job, and ended up staying for the next 30 years!

My career at the Alamo National Bank was a wonderful experience. My boss turned out to be the former Commander of the U.S. Ninth Army, General William H. Simpson....a grand old gentleman.

CHAPTER 12: Epilogue

Douglas Campbell, 94th Fighter Squadron "Hat in the Ring." Campbell was the first "ace" of the 94th FS in World War I. Jack Ilfrey, on the right, was the first "ace" of World War II.

Full Circle

For the last 20 years I have been quite active in the 20th Fighter Group Association. I have been the Group's Newsletter Editor since 1982. Our Group was formed in 1980 and had it's first Reunion in Orlando, Florida the same year.

Since that time our organization has funded and dedicated a permanent Memorial at the sight of the Kingscliffe Airbase. We continue to gather every year in different parts of the United States. We have also organized trips back to England and Russia. But no other trip meant more to me than the visit I made to England in July of 1992.

I was the representative of the 20th Fighter Group Association along with Woody Wilkinson, and Jack and Evelyn George (Associate Members), and their friend Stan Thomas and Nan Roberts (wife and daughter of the late Dr. Paul Roberts, 79th Fighter Squadron Flight Surgeon) and our oldest Member, at 90 years old, Charles Salter.

Also in attendance were members of the 8th Air Force Memorial Museum Foundation; John Greenwood, Francis "Gabby" Gabreski (56th FG), Merle Olmsted (357th FG), Gerald Johnson (56th FG), and Denny Scanlon.

We were invited to a reception at St. James Palace given by the British American Forces Dining Club (organized during the War) honoring the 50th Anniversary of the arrival of the 8th Air Force Army Air Corps Units. It was a grand occasion with Prince Andrew (a jolly good fellow) in attendance and around 600 guests.

We met the other arrivals the next morning at Heathrow Airport. Our group was bused to Cambridge to stay at the *University Arms Hotel*—a most delightful four star hotel. We started to hear-

Kingscliffe Airfield Memorial Dedication Ceremony, August 25, 1983.

Happy Jack's Go Buggy - A Fighter Pilot's Story

Duke of Gloucester and Air Marshal Johnnie Johnson, Britain's top surviving ace of WWII at the Kingscliffe Airfield Dedication Ceremony, August 1983.

Fighter Collection's **P-38J wearing my markings. Note: A very "Happy Jack."**

ing, "The Yanks are Back....The Yanks are Back...." The English people were very happy to see us return after a half a century. No longer did we hear "The Yanks are overpaid, over-sexed, and over here...." When I was England in 1942 and again in 1944, I had the hardest time trying to explain that I was not a "Yank", but a '' Rebel" so I didn't even try this time.

A few minutes away from Cambridge is the Imperial War Museum at Duxford. Duxford airfield has a long glorious history dating back to the First World War. During World War II it was used by the Royal Air Force, it soon became a principle airfield during the weaning days of the conflict in 1940-1942. It was later turned over to the 78th Fighter Group, 8th Air Force, U.S.A.A.F., which occupied the base until 1945.

Today Duxford appears virtually the same as it did during the war. It is the home of one of the finest collections of historic aircraft in the world. One of the most exciting parts of the Imperial War Museum at Duxford is the *Fighter Collection*. It is actually a flying museum. The collection of World War II aircraft all are air worthy.

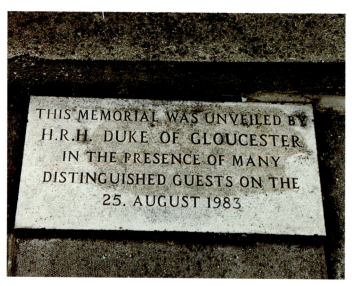

Dedication Plaque at Kingscliffe Memorial.

Duxford Airshow, July 4, 1992. Left to Right - HRS Prince Andrew - Patron of the Airshow, Steven Gray, owner of P-38, Jack Ilfrey, Johnnie Johnson, top surviving British ace (38).

CHAPTER 12: Epilogue

Fighter Collection's **P-38J at its premiere public flight, July 4, 1992. I have never seen a more beautiful sight.**

The "office" of the *Fighter Collection's* P-38.

My visit to Duxford was to be a very special one that day. The Museum Director had just completed the restoration of a Lockheed P-38J. Not only was it a complete and meticulous restoration, but it was painted in my markings! The museum did a remarkable job of duplicating the original markings of "MC-0." Yellow spinners, a highly polished nose, (to give a droop-snoot appearance), and emblazoned on the side of the aircraft was the name "Happy Jack's Go Buggy." I have to admit, the first time I saw the aircraft, it nearly took my breath away.

On July 4th, 1992 it took to the sky for the first time in a public air display. Stephen Gray, the owner of the Fighters Collection, is an accomplished pilot of vintage aircraft in his own right. He had all of four hours of time in the P-38 before taking it up for the July 4th Classic Air Display at Duxford.

Believe me, he flew it in the true manner of a World War II combat fighter pilot. Diving down, buzzing the field, pulling up into a slow roll, on up into a half loop, rolling out at the top. It was the most beautiful sight that I have ever seen.

My first impression was one of pure euphoria. I was mesmerized by it's looks and it's sound. I cannot exactly explain my next impression. As I watched this beautiful machine soar through the heavens, three youthful faces flashed at me. They were the faces of my three good friends and combat partners, whom I had personally seen get killed - Sid Pennington, Dick McWherter and Bill Lovell. I could not stop, nor did I want to, from shedding a few tears.

Also, the fact that Stephen was wearing the pair of gloves that I wore the day I was shot down over France June 13, 1944, brought back that scene of near death.

Fifty years had gone by awfully fast. Reality returned and I thoroughly enjoyed the show. It was the best airshow that I had ever seen. The thought occurred to me,

"Why did I survive?" Perhaps the name that should be emblazoned on the side of that P-38 should now be called "Lucky Jack's Go Buggy."

I remarked afterwards that if Stephen Gray had been one of our replacement pilots even with low P-38 time, he would have definitely been placed on my wing.

A few years later the Fighter Collection's P-38 was repainted as "California Cutie", another P-38 from the 20th Fighter Group. They painted it in an Olive Drab scheme so that the aircraft would not require the maintenance upkeep that a natural metal aircraft needs. Held in July 1996, the Fighter Collection had one of it's premiere airshows of the Season. The P-38, the only flyable example in Europe, was to be one of the main attractions at the show. The Lightning roared down the runway and lifted off for it's afternoon performance. As it came across the field in front of the crowd, it plunged into the ground as it was coming out of a roll. The aircraft cartwheeled in a fiery ball of flame. The pilot, Hoof Proudfoot, did not survive.

Fighter Collection's **P-38 bathing in the English sunshine.**

Woody Wilkinson and Jack Ilfrey.

CHAPTER 12: Epilogue

Fighter Collection's P-38J in all her glory flying over the coast of England.

On the Normandy Beach coast, June 6, 1994. Left to right - Jack Vaileau, Jack Ilfrey, Christianne and Jean Voileau.

At Virginia Bader's at her Costa Mesa Gallery. Left to Right - Art Jeffery, Jack Ilfrey, Hub Zemke, Virginia Bader, and Robin Olds. We joined together to sign prints of Nicholas Trudigan's painting, "Dawn Chorus."

THE WAR PONY
by Buddy Joffrion

Valhalla's gates are opened wide, its portals ever bending.
To receive those men, the sons of Mars, whose lives on earth are ending.
This land alone, for aeons past, receives that mighty horde.
The brave and bold of many lands who have perished by the sword.

There's little new to mark this rite. This the fate intended.
For fighting men to find a home of peace that's never ended.
There's no lament, no hue or cry - the past is all forgotten.
Friend and foe are quick to forget the cause they cast their lot in.

What need to harbor grudge and hate? The fight was grim but just.
The men and arms were even matched—the victor too is dust.
And so it goes, as in ages past, the long thin lines ascending.
The warrior clan still wends its way to the final rest that's pending.

But lo, the scene is changing now - I know not the reason why.
But the tranquil air and happy gait have vanished in the sky.
The marchers now angered much, their wrath they cannot hold.
Though hard to hear, the hate they spill would make one's blood run cold.

With silver wings and jaunty caps, but weary from retreat.
The vanquished German Air Corps strides, embittered, to defeat.
The clamor grows, it's not quite clear, but this I get at least
The thing they hate and fear the most is not a man but beast.

I harkened close, my interest piqued - what can this be they fear?
The battle's done, that life is over - it cannot hurt them here.
At last, I asked, "What is this thing, this thing you loath and fear?"
"The Mustang, friend," they all replied, "Its venom has brought us here."

"This was a war on even terms and fair as wars do go.
Till that devil machine the Fifty-one dealt us its mortal blow.
What kind of craft is this," they said, "that flies for seven hours
And goes so fast it picks the time and place to combat ours?"

"The bombing raids were doomed to fail - the forts were our fair game,
Till those Mustang escorts came along and shot us down in flame.
Our One-0-Nine had held its own - the Focke Wulfs always feared.
But neither could hope to best the foe when that Fifty-one appeared."

"Damn that Schmued and damn his skill - he's the devil's own magician.
We'd send his Mustang straight to hell if we could pick its mission."
And as they entered Valhalla's gates, a voice rang loud and clear.
"If God be just, and I know he must, then there are no Mustangs here!"

COLOR GALLERY

Harry Bisher standing in front of his P-38. Harry was a pilot in the 55th Squadron, 20th Fighter Group. This photo was taken at Kingscliffe, February 1944.

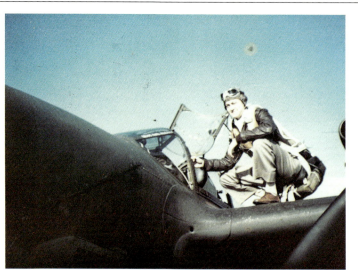

Lt. Chris Pannell on his P-38. Pannell was a pilot in the 55th Fighter Squadron/20th Fighter Group.

Armament shack of the 55th Fighter Squadron at Kingscliffe Airbase. 50 Caliber ammunition boxes can be seen stacked in the tent. The armament personnel took care of our guns and ammo. Seen here basking in the English sunshine are (left to right) Corporal Carl Barlow, PFC Dave Maguin, and Sgt. Wayne Kidda.

Corporal Carl Barlow in front of Lt. Col. Cy Wilson's ship, "Wrangler." Wilson was the Commanding Officer of the 20th Fighter Group until he was shot down in September of 1944.

Line of 79th Fighter Squadron P-51Ds. Kingscliffe, England 1944.

Group of 79th Fighter Squadron Pilots. On the wing (left to right) Brooks Allen, Richard Crawford, unknown, Howard Dailey. Standing (left to right) Ron Berkshire, Bert Beiter, unknown, unknown.

T/Sgt. Howard Hopkins, 79th Fighter Squadron Intelligence kneeling on the wing of Jack Ilfrey's P-51D #44-13831 "Happy Jack's Go Buggy."

Color Gallery

T/Sgt. Howard Hopkins, 79th Fighter Squadron Intelligence, by Ilfrey's P-51D, #44-13831. Note the oversprayed area where the letter "I" is located, and the field-applied olive drab paint covering the top and sides of the fuselage.

Captain William A. Cameron - Flight Leader, 79th Fighter Squadron / 20th Fighter Group sitting on the wing of his P-51D #44-13846, MC-C "Soar Lassie II."

Pilots of the 79th Fighter Squadron (left to right) Lt. James D. Bradshaw, Lt. James H. Baldwin, Lt. Arthur W. Heiden. Kingscliffe, England - September 1944.

Color Gallery

79th Fighter Squadron pilot William A. Cameron (center), and his groundcrew. T/Sgt. Stanley Lecznar (left) and Corporal John C. Henderson (right).

79th Fighter Squadron Ground Officers. Standing (left to right) Captain John S. O'Connell (Personal Equipment), Major Nelson B. Fry (Squadron Executive Officer), Captain Eugene R. Hinkston (Engineering Officer), 1st/Lt. Charles T. Smith (Armament Officer). Kneeling (left to right) 1st/Lt. Orville E. Mintun (S-2 Officer), Captain Arnold E. Heimsath (Chaplain).

Captain Glenn Webb - Flight Leader - 79th Fighter Squadron - 20th Fighter Group, Kingscliffe, England - September 1944. Webb is standing in front of his ship "Glenngary Guy," N. A. P-51DNA #44-13761 MC-Z. Webb named the airplane after his two sons, Glen and Gary.

Color Gallery

The following is a detailed description of the camouflage and markings of the aircraft that were flown by Jack M. Ilfrey in World War II. The artist John C. Valo and I have fully researched these aircraft to the best of our ability.

With the aid of numerous photographs, and detailed information from Jack Ilfrey, we feel that these are the most accurate renderings possible.

It is our hope that these paintings will provide the modeler and historian alike a better understanding to the accurate markings of these beautiful aircraft.

Mark S. Copeland
Editor

COLOR PLATE 1

Lockheed P-38F-1 Serial Number 41-7587 "TEXAS TERROR / THE MAD DASH" 94th Fighter Squadron / 1st Fighter Group 1942-1943

Jack Ilfrey was assigned this P-38F-1 in the United States in 1942. He flew it across the Atlantic Ocean on "Operation Bolero" and kept it throughout his flying career with the **94th Fighter Squadron/1st Fighter Group** in North Africa.

The color plate depiction of the P-38F-1 depicts the markings that it carried when it flew in North Africa in 1942/1943. It was painted in Olive Drab and Neutral Gray, a common finish for U.S.A.A.C. aircraft at that time. The National Insignia on the fuselage boom had a thin yellow surround border ("Operation Torch"), however the yellow surround border was not carried on the top and bottom wing national insignias. The Squadron codes **UN-O** were painted in a white block style on the cooling intakes. The right side of the aircraft also carried these codes, however they were a mirror image of the left side, **O-UN.** The serial number was painted in a standard yellow solid block style on the outboard side of each rudder. The spinner plates were painted in yellow.

The name **"Texas Terror"** was painted in yellow on the left outboard boom. The name was created by Jack, thus giving the origin of his home state away to the enemy! The name the **" The Mad Dash"** was christened by his Crew Chief and was also painted in yellow on the right outward boom. The name came from a serial comic book character that was popular in the 1930's and 1940's.

The aircraft carried 6 swastika victory markings on the left side of the nose section. These were all painted in yellow. The bottom victory marking was half covered with a white rectangle denoting a "half kill." This was applied to the particular victory marking after it was determined that Jack had "shared" a kill with another 1st Fighter Group pilot.

There was also a small "skull and crossbones" painted in yellow on the tip of the nose. Jack also had his name painted on the lefthand side of the fuselage below the leading edge of the wing. This was in cursive writing and was also painted in yellow.

Contrary to some artist's renderings of this aircraft, there was no noseart painted on it. The name, **"Happy Jack's Go Buggy"** never appeared on the airplane.

Color Gallery

COLOR PLATE 2

Lockheed P-38J-15LO 43-28431 "Happy Jack's Go Buggy" 79th Fighter Squadron / 20th Fighter Group —1944

This **Lockheed P-38J-15LO 43-38431** was assigned to Jack Ilfrey while serving in the **20th Fighter Group** at Kingscliffe, England.

The aircraft had an overall natural metal finish with Olive Drab antiglare panels on the top of the forward fuselage section and inboard engine nacelles. The leading edge portion of the engine cowlings and spinners we painted in yellow. The forward portion of the fuselage had a white thin band that wrapped around the entire nose section. Ground crews kept the forward portion of the nose polished to give the appearance of a **"Droop Snoot"** P-38. This was done to try to fool the enemy into believing that the aircraft had a glass nose and was an unarmed reconnaissance aircraft.

A black square, denoting the **79th Fighter Squadron**, was painted on outward side of the rudders with the serial number **328431** painted on the middle third of the square. The inboard sides of each rudder carried a large black **"O"** symbolizing the individual aircraft letter.

The Squadron letters, **"MC-O"** was painted on both sides of the fuselage booms in black. **"MC"** was the identification for the **79th Fighter Squadron**, **"O"** was the individual identification for the aircraft. The Squadron letter codes also were painted on the right side of the aircraft, however they were a "mirror" image of the left, **O-MC**.

Half surround D-Day invasion stripes were carried on the bottom of both booms.

The name **"Happy Jack's Go Buggy"** was painted on the left side of the nose in black letters with a yellow shadowing to the right of each letter. "Top Hat" and "Sweep" mission marks were painted in black. These denoted fighter cover and fighter sweep missions respectively. Eight victory markings were carried on the left side of the aircraft.

These were white discs with black swastikas. There were also two white discs with black silhouettes of locomotive engines. These represented two locomotive engines destroyed.

There was no noseart or victory markings on the right side of the aircraft.

Color Gallery

COLOR PLATE 3

North American P-51D-5-NA Serial Number 44-13761 "HAPPY JACK'S GO BUGGY" September 1944 - December 1944

In July 1944, the **20th Fighter Group** transitioned into P-51s. Jack Ilfrey was assigned P-51D-5-NA Serial Number 44-13761. He flew the aircraft for the remainder of his tour, however, he did not score any victories while flying it. This painting represents the aircraft in the final paint scheme of it's career.

The **20th Fighter Group's** respective Squadrons did not use colored rudders, instead they repeated the aircraft's individual letter in a triangle **(55th FS),** a circle **(77th FS),** and a square **(79th FS).** In the late fall of 1944 the **20th FG** adopted a Group marking of vertical black and white stripes, or "piano keys" on the nose of their P-51s.

Many of the **79th Fighter Squadron** Mustangs were camouflaged with a field applied Olive Drab on the top of the fuselage and the top of the wings and stabilizers. The Olive Drab paint feathered down the sides of the fuselage around the National Insignia and Squadron I.D. Letters in irregular patterns. Black E.T.O. I.D. bands were also carried on the top and bottom of the wings and the stabilizers.

The name **"Happy Jack's Go Buggy"** was first applied to the aircraft in yellow with a red shadowing. Once the Group's black and white I.D. strips ("piano keys") were applied the name was repainted in black with yellow shadowing. The application of the Group's I.D. strips also covered over the mission mark scoreboard that was carried on the aircraft earlier in its career. These comprised of "Sweep" and "Top Hat" symbols, and locomotive "kill" markings. The only evidence of the markings that remained were four bomb mission symbols that were aft of the rear black vertical stripe. The eight "kill" markings were white discs with black swastikas.

The spinner of the aircraft was painted in thirds. The front third was white the aft two-thirds was black. Jack also carried two rear-view mirrors on his canopy. One was factory installed, the other was a mirror off of a British Spitfire, a common sight with numerous **E.T.O.** Mustangs.

The nameboard just in front of the canopy was black with the names in white. This nameboard contained Jack's name and the name of entire aircraft crew. The national markings were painted in a "subdued" application, meaning that the white of the national insignia (star and bar) was a light gray rather than a pure white. The aircraft I.D. codes were in standard black, with the aircraft's individual letter **"I"** in white inside a black square applied to the tail. The aircraft's factory serial numbers were painted out. There was no noseart on the right side of the aircraft.

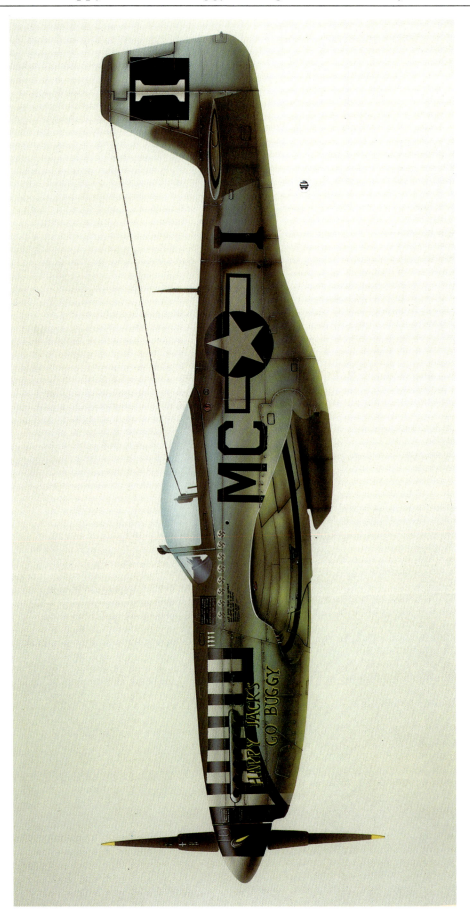

APPENDIX:
Radio Interview with Winston Burdett to CBS, New York
March 21, 1943

MARCH 21, 1943
AT: 18:31 GMT
BURDETT: "Off the Tunisian Coast yesterday, American P-38 Lightning fighters shot eleven enemy planes clear out of the sky. All of our fighters came home. The P-38s have been ringing up all sorts of records out there, and tonight two of the men who fly them are back here at Headquarters (12 Air Force), right in this studio, in fact, to tell how they do it.... they are Jack M. Ilfrey of Houston, Texas and Thomas A. White of Kelso, Washington.
BURDETT: Jack, I hear you've bagged quite a few enemy planes since last November.
ILFREY: Well, I've shot down six, and Tom here has got six also. As a matter of fact, they tell me that's the top score for this front.
BURDETT: Yes, that's so. How do you like flying the P-38?
ILFREY: It's the best fighter we have around here...
BURDETT: Why do you think that?
ILFREY: Lots of fire-power....and speed. And I like the idea of having two engine with me out there....I'm much surer to get home. I had to fly back from Gabes once with many holes in my plane and one engine gone....
BURDETT: Tom, how do you find the P-38 stands up to the Messerschmitt 109 and the new Focke-Wulf, the Germans are flying?
WHITE: We can run circles around them... Up to a certain height, anyway... And I know we're a lot faster because once three Focke-Wulfs chased me half way home from Bizerte but they could never really get near me... The only time the Messerschmitt can beat us on speed is when it is coming down in a dive. The Jerries always hang around on top...and always try to jump the last man, and that's when you've got to be careful.
BURDETT: What do you do then?
WHITE: There's only one thing to do. You whip around to meet them with all your guns wide open.... Most of our work now is escorting bombers, so we don't go around looking for trouble. We wait until the Jerries attack and then we pile up on them.
BURDETT: Jack, as one of the top-scorers on the Tunisian front, what do you think of German pilots?
ILFREY: Sometimes I think that they're either inexperienced or they've got a lot of guts... They're definitely good. And my impression is that the general run of the mill pilots has been getting better since we got here.... But the point is this, we've been learning a lot, too, about how to shoot them down. Our score is several times better today than it was when we started... The Germans have put their best men and their best stuff against us, but right now it's our side setting the pace.
BURDETT: Thanks a lot Jack....and Tom. This is Winston Burdett in North Africa, returning you to CBS, in New York.

BIBLIOGRAPHY

Butcher, Captain Harry C., USNR. (Naval Aide to General Eisenhower). *My Three Years With Eisenhower: The Personal Diary*

Blake, Steve. *King's Cliffe Remembered.*

Doolittle, Gen. James H., with Carroll V. Glines. *I Could Never be so Lucky Again: An Autobiography.*

Freeman, Roger. *The American Airman in Europe.*

Gallagher, Wes. *Back Door to Berlin.*

William Hess, Chris Shores, and Hans Ring, *Fighters Over Tunisia*

Los Angeles Times, February 25, 1942

Pyle, Ernie. *Here Is Your War.*

Rickenbacker, Eddie. *Fighting The Flying Circus*

Toole, O.E.. *World War II Times,* September 1989.

INDEX

1st Pursuit Group 15
79th Fighter Squadron
    64, 65, 66, 69, 70, 72, 83, 87, 92, 93, 95, 103, 112, 113, 114, 115, 116, 119, 121
94th Fighter Squadron 25, 45, 48, 50, 99, 100, 103, 117

A
Agirdir 54, 55
Algiers 35, 40, 42, 54, 56, 59
Ayr 23, 24

B
BOLERO MISSION 17
Bolero Mission 16, 19, 21, 23, 35

C
Carpenter, Jesse 74, 101
Clark, Frank 68

D
Dieppe 28, 34

G
Garman, Ralph 15, 52, 53
Goose Bay 17, 19
Greenland 18, 19, 20, 21, 22

H
Harman, Jim 25, 38, 40, 52
Hat-in-the-Ring 24, 34, 61, 100
Honey bucket 22
honey bucket 22

I
Ibsley 27, 32

K
Kirton-in-Lindsey 25, 26, 27, 28, 33, 34, 35

M
March Field 11, 15, 63
McWherter, Dick 18, 20, 25, 45, 50, 105

N
Neale, Bob 25, 29, 35, 40, 46, 48, 50, 52

O
Oran 34, 35, 36, 38, 39, 40, 41, 55, 59, 62

P
Painton, Frederick C.
Pennington, Sid 21, 25, 105
Piccadilly Circus 31, 32, 33, 69
Pyle, Ernie 49, 50

R
Reykjavik 19, 22, 23
Rickenbacker, Eddie 6, 14, 34, 43, 61
Robert, Jacques 76, 82
Roberts, Newell 14, 15, 25, 27, 42, 52, 53, 54

S
Shahan, Elza 23
Silvers, Roy 25, 27, 44, 50, 100
Starbuck, Donald 25, 29, 52, 54
Stearman PT13 11

T
Tafaroui 40, 41, 42
Tom Cat Black 19

U
Umphries, Everett 16

W
Warrick, Tom 12
White, Thomas 56

Also from the publisher

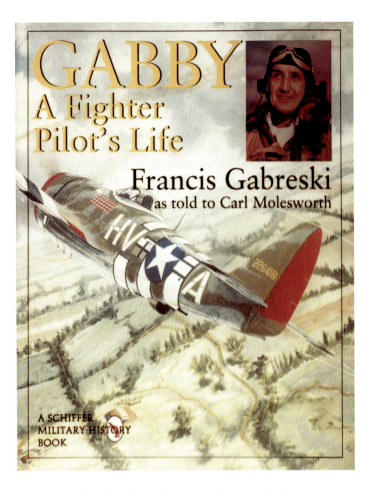
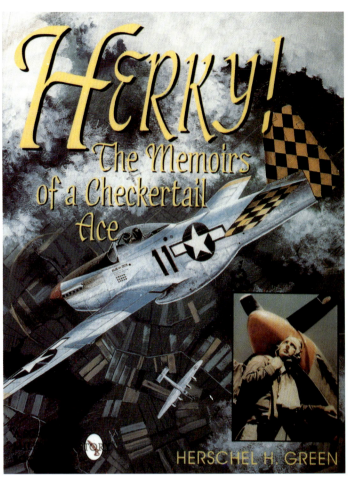

GABBY: A Fighter Pilot's Life
Francis Gabreski as told to Carl Molesworth

This is the full story of Gabby Gabreski, told in his own words. Gabreski's life is a classic American success story. Born to Polish immigrant parents in 1919, he nearly washed out of Notre Dame and then flight school. Now, drawing on his private documents and photographs, Gabby, along with writer Carl Molesworth, tells his thrilling eyewitness story with a candor and a vivid style that should earn this brave pilot a whole new generation of admirers.
Size: 8 1/2" x 11"
over 200 b/w photographs, eight color aircraft profiles
176 pages, hardcover
ISBN: 0-7643-0442-9 $45.00

HERKY!
THE MEMOIRS OF A CHECKERTAIL ACE
Herschel H. Green

The life story of one of the legendary USAAF fighter pilots of World War II who fought across the skies over the Mediterranean and southern Europe in the great aerial campaigns against the Luftwaffe. By the time Colonel Green was grounded by orders of higher headquarters, he was the leading ace of the 15th Air Force with eighteen aerial victories.
Size: 8 1/2" x 11"
over 150 b/w photographs
192 pages,
hard cover
ISBN: 0-7643-0073-3 $45.00